0937925

3/76

7.50

D0844349

An Auto Worker's Journal

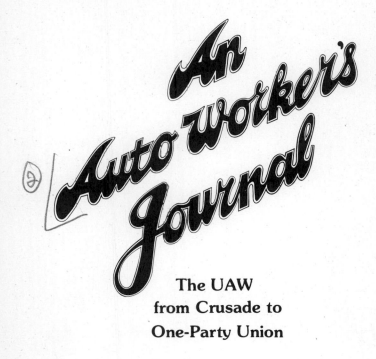

An Auto Worker's Journal

The UAW
from Crusade to
One-Party Union

Frank Marquart

WITHDRAWN FROM UNIVERSITY OF PENNSYLVANIA LIBRARIES

The Pennsylvania State University Press
University Park and London

Library of Congress Cataloging in Publication Data

Marquart, Frank, 1898—
    An auto worker's journal. Bibliography: p. 162
1. Marquart, Frank, 1898—   2. International Union. United Automobile, Aerospace
and Agricultural Implement Workers of America.
I. Title.
HD6509.M37A33   331.88'12'920924 [B]   75-11993
ISBN 0-271-01196-3

Copyright © 1975 The Pennsylvania State University
All rights reserved

Designed by Andrew Vargo

Printed in the United States of America

Photographs courtesy of the Archives of Labor History
and Urban Affairs, Wayne State University.

HD
6509
M37
A33

Contents

Death in the Family • Leisure
Joe Brown • Briggs Strike
Direct Action • FDR Intervenes
Barricades • First Convention
Goodbye to Iola

Preface

Let me begin by explaining the purpose of this labor journal. Recently a United Auto Workers (UAW) International representative said to me: "Why don't you write your memoirs? You've been active in union work for over thirty years. You know the history of the UAW from the early organizing days to the present time. You participated in the great sit-down strikes in the thirties in Detroit and Flint. Old-timers like you have a story to tell. One by one you seniors are passing away, and your experiences and memories will pass away with you unless you record them. Think it over—and don't just think about it, but do it!"

Of course he was right. Those of us who have been so intimately involved in union events over the years ought to record our experiences, observations, impressions, and reflections. And this is what my labor journal will be: a forthright personal account of labor developments as they touched my life. Actually I have already told my story in small part in the form of an oral history recorded on tape now in the Wayne State University Labor Archives. I have also written articles about UAW events for *Dissent, The New Leader, The Socialist Call,* and *The New Republic.* I will never cease to regret that I did not cooperate with Joe Brown (more about him later) when he repeatedly asked me to collaborate with him on writing a history of the UAW based on the wealth of resource material he had collected over many years. I kept putting him off with: "Joe, when I retire we'll make our history a major project—our opus!" Years before I retired Joe died and his widow sold his valuable collection to the Wayne State University Labor Archives. So instead of writing a history of the UAW, I am simply telling about my working life and my union activity, especially in the area of workers' education.

I am grateful:
To Emmy Rosdolsky and Harry Chester for encouraging me to get started. To Iris and Stanford Ovshinsky for bringing my manuscript to the attention of professional personnel in the publishing business. To

Roberta McBride, Philip Mason, and Warner Pflug for assisting me in finding pertinent clippings, newspapers, and pamphlets in the Wayne State University Labor Archives. To the following people who helped me with valuable criticism and suggestions for improving content and structure: Stanley Wier, Virgil Vogel, Staughton Lynd, Martin Glaberman, John Pickering, John Schidman, and Charles Craypo. To many rank and file union local militants who supplied much of the information woven into this book.

 **Introduction**

Chapters 2 to 5 of this journal are about my early life as an auto worker and my radical activities during the 1920s and early 1930s. In the remaining chapters I highlight my experiences in workers' education. In this section the material is not arranged chronologically but is more like an oral history. It consists of different themes, each conveying something about the development of the UAW from a truly democratic union to a one-party state. The themes are based on events that I experienced directly or observed at first hand as well as some that were told to me by workers who experienced them.

The events are like flashes on a screen, instantly conveying an idea of the factors that molded the UAW into the kind of union it has become. Many different elements contributed to this molding process: radical parties, independent militants, idealists, careerists, changes in union structure, and institutionalized collective bargaining.

For twenty years I was engaged in labor education at the local union level, and after that I performed ad hoc educational assignments that brought me in contact with workers at the local union level. So my perspective is from the bottom up and not from the top down. My outlook was shaped by close contact with the rank and file and not in the union bureaucracy far removed from the rank and file.

The events described in this book tell something about how the rank and file acted in the early days when they controlled the union; how the Socialists, Communists, Trotskyites, and other radicals performed in relation to the rank and file; how workers' education was emasculated at the rank and file level; how stewards were deprived of power to settle grievances; how the international union's power structure manipulated and alienated the rank and file from the union. In short, I throw the spotlight on significant phases that illustrate the course the union has taken over the years.

Time was when the American labor movement was respected as a force for social justice. Certainly this view was widely held in early CIO (Congress of Industrial Organizations) days. Today, however, even liberals regard unions as bureaucratized self-interest establishments that no longer identify, as the labor movement once did, with the oppressed and underprivileged sections of the working class. (The exception is Cesar Chavez's United Farm Workers Union, which is a social movement.)

I know many former radicals who admit they have given up on the American working class. I do not share this dark pessimism. I was an auto worker when auto workers were mute, unorganized wage slaves, and "labor experts" wrote magazine articles to prove that auto workers could never be organized. Then came the CIO upsurge that smashed the open shop and forced auto barons to the bargaining table. And I have seen how the rank and file lost control until their union was transformed into a stratified bureaucracy.

But I know this is not the end of the process, for the process is dynamic and periods of relative passivity are followed by periods of spontaneous flare-ups occurring at the point of production. These wildcat strikes are "instinctive" in the sense that the workers themselves are not aware of the logic underlying their action. They are not aware that they are motivated by the logic of workers' control of production. This logic has not yet fully penetrated their consciousness. But that breakthrough in consciousness will come.

Oral History

I could never have written this book without the help of my tape recorder. Every university labor relations department finds the tape recorder indispensable for gathering oral histories—histories that would never come into being without this device. Assembly line workers, lathe hands, miners, steel workers—all men and women who earn their living by manual labor—are not in the habit of writing personal histories. I know how shop stewards often have to be taught how to write even the simplest kind of grievance.

Many times in a Detroit bar called "The Famous" I listened at length to Dodge workers as they told about their working backgrounds. Some of them came from coal regions where they worked in mines; they gave vivid accounts of bitter strikes and deadly union factional battles during the 1920s. I used to ask them: "Why don't you write up those experiences? You could make a lasting contribution to labor history." Invariably the answer was something like this: "Hell, I can't write. Even writing a letter is a pain."

But they find nothing painful about sitting before a tape recorder and pouring out their reminiscences. To appreciate how valuable such oral histories are, read a book like Alice and Staughton Lynd's *Rank and File—Personal Histories by Working Class Organizers.* In their introduction the authors write:

Many famous events in labor history are recounted or alluded to in this book—the Pullman strike of 1894, the McKees Rocks strike of 1909, the steel and packing house strikes of 1919 . . . but these events figure largely as background to the personal development of those who lived through them.

Many notable events in UAW history are recounted or alluded to in the oral histories stored in the Wayne State University Labor Archives in Detroit. Paraphrasing from Studs Terkel's *Hard Times,* one can say that those UAW oral histories "are about Time as well as a time; for some the bell has tolled. Heroes and dragons of a long-gone day were old men, some vigorous, some weary. . . . Some have died." Labor scholars should indeed feel grateful for the tape recorder.

2 Becoming A Radical

My working life began when I was fourteen years old, in the fall of 1913, when my father was laid off from his job in the Westinghouse Electric and Manufacturing Company, East Pittsburgh, Pennsylvania. After vainly seeking work for two weeks, he came home one afternoon and told me: "You've gone to school long enough; tomorrow you quit school and start looking for a job. A lot of kids around here quit school when they were twelve and found jobs; there's no reason why you can't." And he was right. Those were still the days when child labor was common. I was lucky to get as far as the seventh grade. I know kids who hadn't completed more than the third grade when they started to work full time, changing from knee pants to long pants.

It was just as hard for kids to find jobs in the fall of 1913 as it was for their unemployed fathers. I still recall vividly how I searched for work. I went to the employment offices of steel mills, chain mills, glass factories, grocery stores, department stores—wherever I thought I might strike it lucky. Now and then I would get a day's work passing out advertising folders for the A&P or Butler's Grocery Store. For this I earned the munificent sum of fifty cents. Eventually my father landed a job pushing a hand truck in a chain mill in Rankin, near Braddock. Even though he had found work, he saw no reason why I should not find a job also: "You ain't looking for work, you're too damn lazy; you expect me to support you while you bum around." I can still hear his snarling German accent and see the steely look in his eyes and the hatred in his face.

My family was typical of immigrant families of those days. I can't think of a single kid I knew then whose parents did not come from the "old country." And their fathers, like my father, supported their families by hard, unskilled or semiskilled labor, working either a ten-hour shift during the day or a twelve-hour shift during the night. To foremen and higher supervisors in the mills the immigrants were all "hunkies," regardless of their nationality.

My father, six feet tall and as strong as an ox, could be described by the phrase "strong body and weak mind." Our home life was anything but pleasant. Like so many immigrants who worked in the mills, my father took his sufferings and frustrations out on his family. When he left the mill at the end of a shift he headed for a saloon for his whiskey and beer. This was standard practice for mill workers. Sometimes there was more than one round of drinks, and my father came home feeling good—I mean good and mad. He didn't know it, but the hatred he felt for the mill and its slave-driving supervisors was directed against us. He could always find an excuse to pick a quarrel with my mother or to find fault with me, as well as with my sister and brother, who were still little kids. All of us came in for our share, but my mother had to bear the real brunt.

My father's favorite way of letting off steam was to smash dishes by hurling them on the floor. Smashing dishes and roaring curses at us relieved his tensions. I heard that William Faulkner wrote two books about one of his characters, one detailing all the good points about the man, the other describing the evil side of his nature. In the same way I could write at length about my father's savage brutality toward his family; then I could tell how friendly, kind, and even loving he could be toward other people, especially his saloon buddies and their wives and children.

But he wasn't the only one who behaved like that. For a while there lived next door to us in Braddock a Slovakian who worked in the Thompson Steel Mill. Many times my mother and I heard him rave and rant at his wife and little girl, and we heard his wife scream with pain as he beat her. There was a saying in those days: The foremen take their spite out on the mill hands, the mill hands take it out on their wives, the wives take it out on their kids, the kids take it out on the dog, and the dog takes it out on the cat. It seems to me now that drinking and abusing their families were the chief recreations of immigrant mill workers. But this was not universally true, for I can remember some who behaved like decent human beings to their families. I remember how I envied boys of my own age whose fathers played ball with them and were pals to them. Those fathers kept their boys in school until they finished the eighth grade and even, in some cases, sent them to high school!

Five Dollars a Day

My father hated his job as a common laborer in the chain mill and he hated me for not finding a steady job, and life became a living hell for me.

Then came that memorable day in January 1914 when my father came home from work excitedly waving the *Pittsburgh Press* and shouting at us: "Look, in Detroit Henry Ford is paying five dollars a day to all his workers. I'm going to quit my job tomorrow and Frank and me will go to Detroit. We'll both get jobs at Ford's—why we'll be making ten dollars a day, think of it, ten dollars a day!" Then he read aloud excerpts from the front-page story about the Flivver King philanthropist, who was revolutionizing wage scales in America. The more my father talked the more enthusiastic he became.

My mother, however, did not share the enthusiasm. "But how do you know you'll get work in Detroit?," she ventured. I don't recall all that was said but I do remember that her misgivings threw my old man into a rage. He accused her of not cooperating, of not lending moral support; he said she wanted to hold him back. "How to hell can we ever get ahead if you always pull back like that," he demanded, half in German and half in English. While he berated my mother, I picked up the *Press* and read the story for myself. I immediately sided with my father. With the thought of getting away from the hell-hole that was Braddock, of escaping the abuse of my father because I could not find work, of going to a big city—especially a city like Detroit where automobiles were made—I was all for pulling up stakes and heading for the Motor City as soon as possible.

I pointed out to my mother that a number of young men we knew in Braddock had gone to Detroit and found jobs. This was before the five-dollar-a-day Ford announcement. Detroit had a young expanding industry that needed workers of every kind, and employers from that city opened employment offices in East Pittsburgh, offering more money to young workers who could run lathes, milling machines, drill presses, and other machines. I reminded my mother that Charlie Hatchell had gone to Detroit and worked there for over a year, until he made a stake and returned to Braddock. And Cy Burkhardt did likewise. And I mentioned others whose names I no longer remember.

It was agreed that my father and I would go to Detroit, find work at five dollars a day, and send for the rest of the family later. Never, as long as I live, will I forget those days in Detroit in early January 1914! I can't recall how we found the boarding house run by Mrs. Hartlieb on the corner of Lycaste and Waterloo (now East Vernor), but I do recall how we rose early on the following morning, gulped down breakfast, and walked to Jefferson Avenue to take the Jefferson car to Woodward and

In 1913 Henry Ford introduced the moving line to the auto industry. Here at Highland Park, Michigan, the Model T body and chassis were joined.

then transfer to the car that was to take us to the Ford plant in Highland Park.

Nor will I ever forget the sight that greeted our eyes when we walked toward the Ford employment office. There were thousands of job seekers jam-packed in front of the gates. It was a bitterly cold morning and I had no overcoat, only a red sweater under a thin jacket. I don't know how long we stood in that crowd, but I became numb from cold. The crowd kept getting larger and larger and there were angry cries of "for Christ's sake, stop shoving" from men who were near the gates. Some of those men had been waiting there for hours; they were cold, ill-tempered, and in a snarling mood. Several times the company guards ordered the men to stand back and not push against the gates. But those near the gates were pushed by those behind them, who in turn were pushed by those behind them. Suddenly a shout went up—a shout that soon became a roaring chant: "Open the employment office, open the employment office!"

Whether the employment office was ever opened that morning I do not know; whether anyone was hired, I do not know either. But I do know that a man shouted over a megaphone, "We are not hiring any more today; there's no use sticking around; we're not hiring today." An angry roar went up from the crowd: "You sonsabitches, keeping us here all this time and then telling us you ain't hiring, you bastards! . . ." The crowd did not break up; it kept pushing toward the gates. With chattering teeth I suggested to my father that we ought to leave. He cursed me and shouted at me in German that he didn't bring me to Detroit so I could loaf like a bum.

Again the man came with the megaphone: "We ARE NOT hiring today. Go away; no use standing out there in the cold for nothing." And then the ominous warning: "If you don't stop pushing against these gates we're gonna use the firehoses."

I guess everybody thought that was an empty threat made to scare people away. It scared no one. The crowd showed no signs of being intimidated. In fact, it became more unruly. Someone yelled, "Let's crash the goddamn gates!" I can remember how the mood of the crowd suddenly changed; it became ugly, threatening. I heard a roar of approval as someone yelled: "We oughta take down the goddamn place brick by brick." There was shouting and cursing and confusion. Then from those near the gates a cry was raised: "For God's sake the bastards are gonna turn the hoses on us!" Someone near me shouted: "Aw, that's bullshit, they wouldn't dare do a thing like that. . . . " He had hardly finished the sentence when the water came, the icy water that froze almost as soon as it landed on our clothing.

The hoses were turned at an angle and moved from side to side so that the spray hit all sections of the crowd. There was a wild scramble to get away; some people were pushed down and trampled. Several fist fights broke out when some workers shoved those ahead of them. My father cursed, in the way he always cursed when infuriated, his curses beginning in English and rising to a crescendo in German. But he was lucky; the water did not soak through his overcoat as it soaked through my jacket and sweater. By the time we were able to board a Woodward streetcar I was shivering from head to foot.

My father said it was a "Jew plot." A rabid anti-Semite long before Hitler arose to horrify the world, my father said Ford was a Jew and what we suffered that morning was the result of a "dirty Jew trick." When I suggested that "Ford" was not a Jewish name, he told me not to be stupid: "Don't you know Jews change their names for business reasons!"

Among the workers who quit their jobs at Westinghouse and went to Detroit to find work at higher wages was Otto Azinger, whom my father had known for years in Braddock. When we came to Detroit he was a production foreman in the Metal Products Company, a parts plant specializing in the manufacture of automobile axles for the Hudson Motor Company and other auto makers. Otto hired my father to operate a radial drill press, drilling axle shafts. At first he hated the work. He came home from work with his hands swollen and scarred from the hot chips encountered in the drilling. He talked nostalgically about the pleasant job he once had at Westinghouse; he rued the day he came to Detroit and roundly cursed Henry Ford. But what aggravated him most was that he had to work and I could not find a job.

Every day I made the factory rounds—Chalmers, Lozier, Continental Motor Company, Packard, Zenith Carburetor, and a host of small parts plants that have long since vanished from Detroit's East Side. Everywhere I received the same answer: "No, we are not hiring today." The hiring agent of the Detroit Nut and Bolt Company told me: "Hell, kid, you're too skinny to run any of them machines we got in there."

Every evening when my father came home from work he asked me where I had looked for work; I told him, but he simply did not believe me: "You didn't look for work, you bummed around. Why to hell should you work when the old man's working? That's what you think, ain't it?" And so on and on. He was too ignorant and brutal to understand that the worst thing a father can do to a boy is to crush his pride and self-respect. He made me feel that I couldn't find a job because of some fault within myself. Once one of the boarders told him at the supper table: "Don't blame the boy because he can't find work; today if you want to get a job, it's not what you know or how good you are—it's who you know." Then he added: "Isn't that how you got your job—through someone you know?" I gave my father a meaningful look. He fidn't say anything.

The Stopwatch

And that was how I finally obtained my first job in Detroit—through someone my father knew, the employment manager of the Metal Products Company, another former employee of Westinghouse. Through him I got a job in the office—and lasted about ten days. I had to address envelopes by hand, make out requisitions, distribute daily mail in the various departments of the plant, and take care of office supplies. I had neither the required education nor the experience to do the work competently. I was too slow in addressing envelopes and I lacked the knack of working out a system for handling supplies. One day the supervisor called me into his office and told me that the job was too much for me; they would have to get another boy, one with some high school education. He said I would not be laid off but transferred to a factory job on the fourth floor. The office job paid thirty dollars a month; the factory job paid ten cents an hour, ten hours a day, five and a half days a week.

And so began my life as a factory hand, working "on the bench" filing castings and ring gears, grinding the burrs off nuts on a small power-driven emery wheel. Now that both my father and I had jobs, we sent for my mother, sister, and brother and rented a house on Fisher Avenue near Jefferson. In those days the Detroit River came all the way up to Jefferson Avenue in that area, and I can still remember the horse-drawn dump wagons unloading trash, little by little filling in the river and creating new land on which the Whittier Hotel, the River House, and other high-rise structures would eventually be erected.

My mother was a good German cook and in no time we had a house full of boarders, all young workers who came to Detroit from East Pittsburgh, Oak Hill, Turtle Creek, and Braddock. The East Side section of Detroit from Hart Avenue to Fairview was known as "Little East Pittsburgh." In Metal Products, former Westinghouse workers were running lathes, gear cutters, screw and other machines. The management introduced a piecework system, and my father began to boast that he was earning at least 25 percent more than he could earn at Westinghouse. He was happy now with his job, as I was with mine. I asked for a raise and my pay was increased by 50 percent, that is, to fifteen cents an hour. But that was not what made me happy. The hourly rate did not mean anything once piecework became established.

Piecework turned me into a rebel. The class struggle? Conflict between capital and labor? I had not heard such talk and would not have known what it meant even if I had heard it. About social conditions I was an illiterate. The only items I read in newspapers were the funnies and the sports page. Magazines? I doubt if I knew the difference between a slick monthly and a cheap pulp. I had about as much theoretical knowledge as a country clod. *And yet I became a rebel!*

I became a rebel out of sheer instinctive, spontaneous experience. The stopwatch did it. The time-study man's stopwatch told me there was a conflict of interest between me and the company. The time-study man was the agent of the company. And the stopwatch was the instrument by which the company got as much as it could out of my hide. So I knew I had to fight the stopwatch.

One day the time-study man came to time me while I was filing lock nuts. The lock nut was about four inches in diameter and my job was to file off the sharp burrs on the edges. When the time-study man stood over me, stopwatch and clipboard in hand, I slowed down every motion I made without seeming to do so deliberately. I reached in the pan with my left hand, picked out a nut, held it in my left hand, and filed with the right. It was the simplest kind of operation and on the basis of my movements the time-study man set a price on the job. Once the price was set I had no difficulty "making out," as the workers used to say. Instead of holding the nut in my hand when filing, I made a "die" by cutting out a form on a board. With the nut held securely in the form I could file with both hands and turn out five nuts in the time it took to turn out one before. It was similar with other jobs: those of us who worked on the bench could find all kinds of shortcuts—ways we never revealed to the time-study man. Although my day rate was only fifteen cents an hour, thanks to piecework I used to bring home from twenty to twenty-five dollars a week, fantastic pay for a kid in those days.

Factory Hand

And so the months went by and I became increasingly conditioned to the ways of a young factory hand. I chummed around with factory workers of my age group—a "peer group," I guess the sociologists call it. After work we went home, ate supper, and met in a bar, usually Premo's on Jefferson Avenue near the car barn (now a police station). Though a minor, I was tall and never got turned down by the bartender when I put my foot on the brass rail and ordered, "Gimme a beer." My ego always inflated when the bartender served me but refused one of my pals because he was shorter and looked younger. In the saloon, men gathered in groups and usually talked shop. Each tried to impress the others with how important his particular job was, how much skill it required.

Saturday night was the *big* night. My pals and I met in Curley's Poolroom on Jefferson Avenue and shot several games of pool. Then we went downtown to take in a burlesque, either the Gaiety or the Cadillac. The Gaiety had a bar downstairs and during intermission we made a dash for the bar and ordered a hamburger with onion and a glass of beer. After the show we went to Champlain Street. How many Detroiters today know where Champlain Street was and what it was noted for in those far-off days? In our circle it was nicknamed "Joy Street." On a Saturday night you could see men forming lines at some of the houses on Champlain Street, with policemen on hand to keep order. Because of its red-light reputation the name of the street was changed to East Lafayette, after prostitution was outlawed during the First World War.

As time went on I discovered that I was working harder and harder for less and less money. We pieceworkers outsmarted ourselves; in the words of Old Sam Johnson, the oldest worker in our department, "we cut our own throats." At first I was so naive that I actually believed the company would allow me to continue earning that high piecework pay. Then I found out why you couldn't win against the company. They retimed one job after another. Then I had to work harder to earn my twenty to twenty-five dollars a week. And they kept cutting the price until I worked much harder to bring home fifteen dollars a week than I did when I made twenty-five dollars. The time-study man used a new system when timing a job. Instead of timing the worker, he took off his coat, rolled up his sleeves, worked furiously for ten or fifteen minutes, and set a time on the basis of his output. Once I told him: "You know damn well you couldn't keep up that pace all day long. How do you expect us to do it?" I remember his answer well: "Look Bud, if you get the rag out of your ass you can make out." And he walked away.

In the spring of 1915 I quit the "Metal" and landed a job running a spindle drill press in the Continental Motor Company on Jefferson Avenue. The economic curve was rising in America. In Europe, armies were being hurled against each other and war orders poured into the United States. More and more of my friends accumulated their stakes and went back to East Pittsburgh or nearby areas and found work at good pay at Westinghouse; some even got jobs in New Jersey factories which were advertising for machine hands at tempting pay rates.

The composition of the work force began to change in Detroit. The automatic conveyor and specialized one-purpose machines were being introduced; production operations were being split up and simplified. The demand for experienced machinists was falling off. Men could be hired off the street and trained to do the specialized operations in a short time. Farm hands, who didn't know a lathe from a hand miller, were hired and trained on production jobs. More and more people with southern accents came into the factories.

Not only were new and faster machines being installed, but assembly operations were replanned and speeded up. When I started to work for Continental, motor assemblers put together a complete motor. They were called "motor builders" and earned good pay. But in time the motors were being assembled on conveyor lines, each man performing only a single task. The emphasis increasingly was on speed, speed, speed. I remember how, in Metal Products Company, a man running a Gleason gear cutter worked on only one machine. While the machine was automatically cutting the gear, the operator sat down leisurely and waited until it was time to insert another gear. In time the man found himself running two machines, then three, then four.

Stealing a Trade

My father, who also quit his job at Metal Products when piece rates on his operation were slashed, blamed it all on Ford: "The Jew Ford pays his men five dollars a day and drives them like slaves, and now the other companies are driving all of us like slaves." In that expanding period of the auto industry it was relatively easy for a young worker to quit a job in one factory and get a job in another place. I know some chaps who actually learned the toolmaking trade that way. A young man hired out in a factory as a toolmaker. He was placed on a machine and, with the help of the man working on the next machine, picked up a little skill—until the foreman discovered that he was a "shyster" and fired him. Then he hired out in another plant, picked up a little more skill, and so on, until he acquired enough competence to hold down a toolroom job. We called it "stealing the trade." Other workers acquired some semiskilled specialty. For example, a lathe hand always made more money than a drill press hand. Thus a shopmate of mine decided he was going to quit his drill press job and become a lathe hand. I recall he was fired from three different places before he acquired enough skill to hold down a lathe job in Chalmers (the old Chalmers plant is now a Chrysler unit on Jefferson Avenue).

In the spring of 1916 I hired out in the Bower Roller Bearing Company as a finish external grinder hand. I didn't even know how to start up the machine. But when the machine setter learned that I came from Braddock, where he had lived for years, he took special pains to teach me how to grind the rollers to the specified size. Many times in later years I wished he had fired me the first day, for grinding was not the proper work for someone with a frail chest like mine.

Looking back, I think I can say that I was a typical young factory worker in those days. I was in every sense what the Industrial Workers of the World (Wobblies) called a "scissorbill." I had about as much social vision as a cow. I had the usual prejudices of a semi-literate American. I had no use for Jews. I remember how gleefully I used to laugh when a burlesque comedian would portray the stereotype Jew. All Negroes were simply "niggers" to me, and I just took for granted that they were a kind of inferior species compared to us whites. I remember how my pals and I reacted to the socialist soapboxers who held forth at Jefferson and Hillger. We lumped them together with the Salvation Army speakers and poked fun at them.

But there was one street corner orator who fascinated us—Railroad Jack. Railroad Jack had quite a reputation as a man with a prodigious memory. He spent hours daily boning up on things in the public library. He earned his living by collecting nickels and dimes at street corners. He called for questions—any questions—and then answered them. It could be a question about the part some general played in the American Civil War, or about the Homestead Steel Strike, or who shot President McKinley and why. Whatever the question, Railroad Jack always could tell you and embellish his answers with interesting details. In later years I was told he challenged student audiences at the University of Michigan to "bring on your questions" and astounded them with his encyclopedic memory.

When America entered the First World War in 1917 I was working at Bower Roller Bearing. Like most typical young American workers I was patriotic, but not so patriotic that I cared to enlist in the Army—and that was true of most of the young fellows in the shop. But when the draft was put into effect a number of us decided to enlist as stretcher bearers. "Better and safer to be a stretcher bearer than a doughboy in the trenches," we said. Among those of us who volunteered to enlist in this branch of the service, all passed the physical tests except me. I was put in class 4-F because of lack of vision in my left eye and curvature of the spine. At first I took my rejection very much to heart; I used to go to the Armory Building on Larned Street and watch enviously as my buddies were being put through their paces by the sergeant.

A labor shortage soon developed during the war and jobs were easy to get. I heard that cylinder grinders in the Continental Motor Company were earning more than a dollar an hour. I quit Bower Roller Bearing and got a job grinding cylinders at Continental. In those days the cylinder bores in motor blocks were ground in specialized Heald machines. The job called for finish precision grinding; the bores had to be smooth as glass and ground to one-thousandth of an inch. It was dry grinding and the cast iron dust was drawn off by a suction blower, but the operator could not escape inhaling some of it—in fact, too much of it.

"Limey"

While I was working at Continental an incident occurred which led to a new phase in my life. One day the supervisor, accompanied by a Liberty Bond salesman, made the rounds from machine to machine to sell bonds. You were not asked if you wanted to buy any; you were asked, "How much can we put you down for?" The bonds came in different denominations from $25 to $100, but I can't remember what sum I signed up for. I do recall that an Austrian worker who was a "learner" on a cylinder grinding machine said flatly that he would not buy any bonds. When pressed by the salesman, he replied in a voice all of us could hear: "I won't buy any of your goddamn bonds and I hope the Allies lose the war. . . ." A number of us rushed at him, threw him to the floor, beat him badly, and poured a can of yellow paint over him—paint that was used by the inspector to mark defective motor blocks. Then we told the supervisor that unless the "hunky" was fired on the spot we would refuse to work. The man was fired and two plant protection men were called to take him out of the plant. He must have been in great pain, for he limped and held his hand over his groin as he was led away, groaning.

Only one worker in that department, an Englishman we called "Limey," did not attack the Austrian or raise his voice when the rest of us served the ultimatum on the supervisor. He worked on the machine next to mine, and when I talked with him about "that hunky traitor" he was noncommittal. He was a married man with two kids, a pleasant chap, well liked by the boys in the department. He was an expert cylinder grinder and taught me several tricks that helped to increase my premium pay.

Working next to each other we had ample opportunity to talk, because it took several minutes to grind each bore in a six-bore motor block, the machine doing the work automatically. One day he asked me a question that I couldn't answer: Why don't the automobile workers have a union? I knew in a vague way what a union was, for I knew carpenters and bricklayers and railroad workers who belonged to unions. He told me that in England all factory workers belonged to unions, and he explained the ABC's of unionism to me. "If we had a union the company could not cut premium rates anytime they wanted to, like they do here," he said. Then he told me the workers in England also had their own political party—a labor party—and he could not understand why the American workers always voted for a capitalist party. "Can you tell me any real difference between the Republican and the Democratic parties?" he asked. In those days I could not have cared less; I was as politically indifferent as I was religiously indifferent.

I was greatly impressed when I discovered that Limey knew more about American history than any of the Americans in that department. He asked questions like: "Why was your American Civil War fought?" I answered, "To free the slaves, of course; everyone knows that." Then he told me that's what he thought I would say, but I was wrong—and he proceeded to explain that the war was a conflict between the slaveholding class in the south and the capitalists in the north.

In this way we discussed one subject after another and more and more I found myself becoming interested in things to which I had been oblivious before. One day he handed me a little booklet, *The Apostate*, by Jack London. It was the story of a boy who slaved in a jute mill, so driven by the speedup that in desperation he quit his job, crawled into a boxcar in the freight yard, and took to the road. It reminded me of how we had to drive ourselves to make out every time piece rates were cut in Metal Products.

I was eager to know if Limey had any more stories by Jack London. He loaned me a short story, "The Dream of Debs," about how the American workers won a major victory by means of a general strike. All

I knew about Eugene Debs up to that time was what the newspapers reported: that he was the leader of the Socialist Party, a party that was all-out against the war. I argued that Debs should be put in jail and the party deserved to be outlawed. Limey was cagey. He told me he never argued with people about their patriotism or their religion, that he respected my right to think as I did, and all that sort of thing. But a few days later he handed me an article cut out of some magazine, consisting of excerpts of a speech made by President Woodrow Wilson to the effect that all modern wars are fought over commercial interests. Such was his technique: when he broached a subject with which I violently disagreed, he would talk about something else—and later hand me a newspaper clipping or magazine story that would bear out his viewpoint.

My respect for the guy grew. I told myself he was not a "bullshitter" like the others. Once he invited me to his home for Sunday dinner. I still have pleasant recollections of that visit. He showed me his shelf of books. I went away with Jack London's *Iron Heel* under my arm. I read the book over and over; in fact I can say I acquired the habit of reading thanks to Jack London. At Limey's suggestion I applied for a public library card and took out more books by Jack London. I enjoyed *Martin Eden*, a fictionalized autobiography, so much that I bought a copy. What a change in consumer preferences! To spend money for a book instead of spending it in a poolroom or a saloon! Clearly my attitudes were evolving.

Young Socialists

At Limey's suggestion I attended my first Young Socialist meeting—a debate between a local preacher and Arthur Lewis, Socialist writer and lecturer from Chicago. It was as exciting as a prizefight. The hall must have been filled mostly with Socialists; they cheered and clapped wildly for Lewis and damned the preacher with faint applause. From the time he began to speak, I was fully prejudiced in favor of Lewis. He argued that organized religion was bad because it tried to make people more concerned about getting pie in the sky after they die than about improving conditions for everybody in this world.

After the debate Limey introduced me to some of his Socialist friends. We went to a bar for beer and pretzels. They talked, I listened. It was like a postmortem of the debate, especially of the preacher's arguments. They picked his points to pieces. They were factory workers, like I was, but they knew so much more than I did. One of them, a screw machine hand at the Packard Motor Company, told me he was the literature agent in Branch 1 of the Detroit Socialist Party. "We hold classes there; why don't you drop around sometime?," he invited. And I did, the following Sunday morning. A tall man with a slight Swedish accent was conducting a class in "Socialism, Utopian and Scientific," by Friedrich Engels. On that day they were taking up the section on metaphysics and dialectics. It was Greek to me. The instructor called on one person to read a paragraph, then he reread it and asked the person called upon to explain it. When he asked me to read a paragraph I wanted to crawl into a hole. I stammered, stumbled over words, blushed, and was so embarrassed that I wished to hell I hadn't come near the place. The instructor was tactful; rather than call on me to explain what I read, he said it was one of the most difficult paragraphs in that section of the book and he proceeded to explain it.

I do not remember how many attended that class, but I do know that the majority were young people, around my age. I marveled at the way some of them could explain the paragraphs they read. When I told Limey after the class how smart I thought they were and how ignorant I was, he laughed and told me that some of those people belonged to the Young People's Socialist League and had been attending classes for several years, "ever since they stopped wearing knee pants." Then he told me that a more elementary class was being conducted on the East Side of Detroit—Mary Marcy's "Shop Talks on Economics." "You'll like that class," Limey said, "and you'll like the instructor, a guy by the name of Al Renner."

Limey was right. I did like the class, because Mary Marcy in her pamphlet explained the principles of economics in ways that related directly to my experiences in the factory. I liked the instructor, too. Al Renner was a tall, massively built man, who was later to make quite a name for himself in union and radical circles of Detroit. His manner of conducting the class made me feel at ease. I read and reread the pamphlet at home and looked forward to those Wednesday evening sessions so I could show off my knowledge.

With new attitudes came new interests. I remember Limey saying to me one day: "When I first knew you, you were a scissorbill; now you're class conscious." I regarded that as a high compliment, and it inflated my ego. I considered myself as somehow superior to my shopmates who were "scissorbills," and I deplored their ignorance. This kind of arrogance was not uncommon among radicals.

I felt flattered when people called me a radical. A little knowledge is a dangerous thing; I thought I had all the answers and adopted a supercilious tone toward those who differed with me. I gave up the pool hall for radical meetings. I did not know the difference between the Socialist Party, the Industrial Workers of the World, and the Socialist Labor Party, and I attended their meetings indiscriminately. I couldn't figure out why they could never get together, since they strived for the same goal—the classless society. I became more confused when splits took place in the Socialist Party after the Russian Revolution. By that time the radicals in Detroit owned the "House of the Masses," a large structure with many halls and rooms, at the corner of Gratiot and St. Aubin. No matter when you went there you could always count on a lecture or a class or a group argument taking place. Sometimes those events took place simultaneously.

Every Sunday afternoon there was a lecture. Sometimes a local speaker was featured, but most of the time outside speakers, who drew larger audiences, were scheduled. I can't remember most of their names, but in that period (1918) I heard Scott Nearing, Kate Richards O'Hare, Charles Ruthenberg, Eugene Debs, Big Bill Haywood, to mention only a few. The Socialist Party had many foreign federations and most of those who came to listen to radical speakers were foreigners.

Among those who spoke were writers and travelers who had been in Russia during or shortly after the Bolshevik Revolution. They described the revolution in glorious terms: the heroism of the people in the face of counterrevolution, the genius of men like Lenin and Trotsky, the seizure of the land by the peasants and of the factories by the workers, the rooting out of the last vestiges of capitalism, and the steady building of a workers' world, free from human exploitation of man by man. I think now that many in the audience must have been Russian and Slavic nationalists. Every time a speaker championed Bolshevik achievements they applauded wildly, cheered loudly, and stamped their feet until the rafters shook. It was like a religious revival meeting. I "got religion," too. Those sessions were like an emotional spree for me. I was just as sure as the others in the audience that a brave new world was being created in Russia. And when the speaker drew an ominous picture of how the European and American capitalists were out to strangle the Russian Revolution I booed and hissed as loudly as the others.

Federal Raids

In the shop I got into many arguments about the Russian Revolution. Some of my shopmates believed what they read in the papers—that Lenin had been bought off by German gold to keep Russia out of the war and that the Bolsheviks were underground conspirators, a bunch of anarchists who wanted power for themselves. I defended the revolution with all the catch phrases and generalities I had heard in the House of the Masses. I didn't know the difference between Bolsheviks and Mensheviks, except that one meant minority and the other majority. I was utterly ignorant of the programmatic differences between the Bolsheviks and the Social Revolutionaries. Yet I argued in such a tone of cocksureness that I acquired a reputation among the workers in my department of being well-informed about what's going on in Russia. And everyone in the department, including the foreman, took for granted that "Marquart's a Red, he attends meetings in 'Dynamite Hall,'" as they called the House of the Masses.

One Sunday when I attended a lecture, federal agents swooped down on the House of the Masses to look for "slackers." This happened frequently in Detroit (and I suppose other cities, too) in 1918. Federal agents raided dance halls and other places where young men gathered; the men were lined up and asked to produce their draft cards. Those who could not produce cards were taken to the federal building for investigation. Many Socialists and war objectors refused to be drafted and served one year in jail as a result. Others refused to register and did not even have draft cards. When caught, they were in real trouble. The federal agents acted as if they were convinced that all foreigners and radicals were traitors. They herded us in the large hall like cattle. They didn't even look at our draft cards closely. Those who produced cards were told, "Okay, you can go."

The YPSL (Young People's Socialist League) girls were a big help on that particular Sunday. For example, one of them borrowed my card after I got out of the hall; then she went back into the hall, moved slowly among those who were still lined up, and asked: "Who needs a draft card?" I was told that several men succeeded in eluding arrest, thanks to the rebel girls.

Armistice Day—11 November 1918—never will I forget. I was working in the shop when the news broke. The workers went wild. They pounded on steel tables with machinist hammers; they danced and yelled like banshees. In my department someone yelled, "Let's go to Toledo and celebrate!" Michigan was a dry state then; Ohio was still wet. Those of us who did not have cars rode with those who did. The crowds on the streets were shouting, dancing, waving flags, and yelling: "Hock the Kaiser, Hock the Kaiser!" It was the same in Toledo as in Detroit, as it was in every other city. Men in Army or Navy uniforms were the luckiest of all. They were literally mobbed by young girls. In Toledo we went to the nearest saloon and got drunk. Then we went up and down avenues, mingling with the crowds, engaging in all sorts of crazy antics.

With the end of the war came the end of wartime prosperity. The first to be laid off in the production departments were women who were hired during the war, when male workers were in short supply. Next the plant went down to three days a week and workers were laid off in droves. Early in January 1919 I received a letter from a man who used to board with us in Detroit. He was now a foreman in the piston grinding department in the Chandler Motor Company in Cleveland. He offered me a job and told me I could make good money at piecework. I was lucky enough to be able to work full time that winter.

I soon discovered that Cleveland had a lively Socialist movement. The Party sponsored weekly lectures, similar to those held in the House of the Masses. Every speaker flayed capitalism and hailed the Bolshevik Revolution. The Western capitalist powers were condemned for supporting the White counterrevolution. And all the speakers sounded the hopeful note: "There will be a soviet revolution in Germany, France, England, and eventually in America." I knew nothing about the ideological differences among Socialists then. I knew there were factions, but I knew nothing about the issues that divided them. I attended a study class conducted by a group of young Socialists. The text was *Mass Action*, by Louis C. Fraina. (I did not know then that in later years he would become Professor Lewis Corey at Antioch College and that I would engage him to conduct a course in economics for the UAW summer school at Lakeport, Michigan.) All I got out of that YPSL class was the general impression that some day soon the working class would rise up spontaneously, instinctively, in one momentous mass upsurge to overthrow capitalism and establish a Soviet America. It was all so very simple and so utterly inevitable. It never dawned on me to question this article of faith, despite the fact that the workers with whom I came in contact in the shop were all good 100 percent patriots. I used to dismiss them contemptuously as "scissorbills."

I know now that we pro-Soviet enthusiasts had our heads in Russia and romanticized about conditions existing in the United States. Every time I attended a lecture I came away with a stack of literature under my arm: papers, pamphlets, even a book occasionally. Today I wonder how much I understood of what I read in those days. Each of the different factions put out a paper of some kind. I read them all, and they all seemed convincing. I attended lectures the way a devout Catholic attends church services. I was a zealot; socialism was my religion. Yet if anyone had called me religious I would have felt insulted. Didn't Marx say that "religion is the opiate of the people"? And whatever Marx said was gospel truth.

Riot!

Winter passed and spring came. The Cleveland Socialists, under the leadership of Charles Ruthenberg, were preparing for a gigantic May Day parade. Socialist branches in different parts of the city were getting ready for the occasion. Parades were held in the evening. With little red flags pinned on our coat lapels we marched down Euclid Avenue. These weekly parades were dress rehearsals for the big parade to come on 1 May. I will never forget that day as long as I live. The event was well planned. Each branch was scheduled to meet at a certain section of the city, along the parade route. I was told that Ruthenberg led the parade on a white horse, although I did not see this, since my contingent was at a considerable distance from the front. Men, women, and children marched, four abreast. We carried placards hailing the Russian Revolution, denouncing capitalist exploitation, calling for a Soviet America.

This was at a time when the Russian Revolution sent shivers through conservative circles in America. The infamous Palmer Raids were soon to come. The daily press carried on an unrelenting campaign of slander against Bolshevist Russia. The Red Scare was being whipped up in this country. Servicemen were returning from overseas, and Cleveland, like other cities, welcomed them as heroes. One can imagine how the placards, the red flags, and the foreigners in the parade must have made the uniformed servicemen feel that day. And they soon had a chance to act out their feelings.

I don't know how long we marched before the alarmed cries were raised: "The police are breaking up the parade! The police are riding into people, clubbing them right and left!" That day I witnessed mob terror in action. The police used their clubs viciously on heads, backs, and shoulders. Servicemen armed themselves with whatever came to hand and waded into the crowd swinging and slugging. I saw men and women lying prostrate in the street. I saw blood flowing from gashes, the wounded holding their heads in their hands and screaming with pain. I saw a 200-pound, well-dressed businessman bully a teen-age girl: "Take off that red emblem. Take it off before I pull it off. Take it off before I pull off all your clothes, you little bitch!" The girl was so terrorized, her hands were trembling so badly, that she could hardly remove the emblem. I also saw a big burly cop pull a Negro out of the crowd, push him up against a building, and beat him on the head with his fists so furiously and so long that I turned away and retched.

I heard police sirens shriek and a score of patrol cars appeared. The police grabbed those nearest to them and literally threw them into the patrol cars, including the injured. The returned servicemen had a field day. In vigilante fashion, they formed bands and headed for "bolshevik" headquarters. They turned the Socialist Party headquarters into a shambles. Furniture was smashed to bits. Typewriters and mimeograph machines were wrecked and thrown into the street. Books, pamphlets, file cards were torn to bits and scattered outside. The IWW hall and its contents were similarly ruined. So were Socialist branch offices. Whoever happened to be inside was beaten.

The next day I read editorials in Cleveland dailies commending the "returned heroes" for their exemplary service to their country and inviting the Reds to go back where they came from if they did not like America.

When I reported for work, the superintendent, who somehow found out that I was in the parade, fired me. That night I took the D&C liner back to Detroit. Soon I was back on the job, grinding cylinders at the Continental.

Strike

I believe it was in August 1919 that I got my first taste of union activity.

There was a kind of unwritten law among cylinder grinders to turn out no more than twelve six-cylinder blocks in the nine-hour shift, which was then the standard workday in auto factories. We knew that if we turned in more than twelve blocks, management might cut our premium rates. We practiced what the English workers called "ca'canny"—that is, we limited our output. But not every operator obeyed the unwritten law; there were a number of men we called "hungry bastards," who were so greedy for extra pay that they turned in fourteen or fifteen blocks. The inevitable happened: jobs were retimed, premium rates were cut, and we had to turn out extra blocks to make the same pay.

At first all the resentment was directed against the "hungry bastards." They were ostracized; no one would talk with them. Every time one of them went for a drink of water or to the washroom, the belts on his machine were cut, the grinding wheel was smashed, his personal tools were damaged, the word "RAT" was chalked on his machine in block letters. They were treated in the way union building tradesmen treat a scab on the job. I remember that two of the speed kings could not take it any longer and quit Continental. But that didn't help matters, for the premium rates were not restored.

Then one day at noon, when the fellows were sitting in a group eating lunch, Limey came up with a suggestion: "Why don't we form a union of cylinder grinders and demand our old rates back?" It sounded like a good idea. I remember that it caused a lively discussion.

Some of the boys believed that we cylinder grinders were indispensable: "They can't produce motors without cylinder blocks, and they can't use cylinder blocks unless we grind them. Cylinder grinders are always hard to get; they can't hire men off the streets and put them to work grinding cylinders. It takes months before a new guy can get out production, and he could never get out production unless we break him in. If we form a union and refuse to break in new people— the company will be on its ass!" It sounded convincing. Every one of us became enthusiastic over the idea.

At noon the next day, we formed a union right in the department. A committee of three was selected to present our demands to the general foreman of the entire machine division. Limey, one of the committeemen, was named spokesman. The next morning we were all agog when we came to work: we were a union now, we were going to stand together, we were going to present a solid front against the company, and we were sure that we would win our demand, a single, simple demand: "Twelve blocks a day for our former pay." At 9 A.M. the members of the "bargaining committee" shut down their machines and headed for the general foreman's office. As they walked down the aisle the boys urged them on: "Atta boy, fellows, lay it on the line, give it to 'em straight, don't take no for an answer. . . ."

The general foreman made short shrift of the committee. He flew into a rage, rushed over to the department foreman and told him to shut off the electric current that powered the machines, and called all grinder hands to his office. When we gathered in front of the office, the general foreman didn't talk, he barked and frothed at the mouth with anger: "There'll be no premium changes on the cylinder grinding operations, none whatever. This so-called committee is fired, every damn one of them. And those of you who don't like the working conditions here can get to hell out. I want all of you who want to work to go back to your machines; those of you who don't want to work, go to the front office and get your pay. That's all." And he stormed back to his desk.

Five of the men went back to their machines. The rest of us went to the front office for our pay. As we left the department we yelled at those who stayed behind: "Scab! Scab! Scab!"

So ended my first experience with unionism. Little did I dream on that day that the time would come when not only Continental Motors but the entire auto industry would be organized by a powerful union!

3 From Carriages to Autos

The first auto shops were small, and most of the work was done by skilled craftsmen—carriage builders, painters, carpenters, and others. In the early 1900s such workers belonged to the Wagon and Carriage Workers of North America. As automobiles increasingly replaced carriages the American Federation of Labor (AFL) widened its charter and the name was changed to United Automobile, Aircraft, and Vehicle Workers of America. When the union insisted on operating along industrial union lines, it was opposed by such crafts as the machinists, boilermakers, upholsterers, and metal polishers. At the 1917 AFL convention the craft leaders brought their influence to bear and the Auto Workers Union was suspended from the Federation. I heard about this union for the first time shortly after I got fired from Continental Motors. I remember well the first meeting I attended in the union hall. The attendance was small and the speaker, an organizer, explained the difference between craft unions (to which only workers of a certain craft or trade can belong) and industrial unions (to which all workers in a given industry may belong, regardless of occupation or trade).

It was my first real lesson in the ABC's of unionism. From my factory experience I could see the logic of industrial unionism in an auto plant. When I worked in the Continental cylinder grinding department there were times when I could not work on my machine because of a shortage of motor blocks. Then the foreman would put me on another job temporarily. One time it might be buffing and polishing crank shafts, at another time I'd be put on a paint spray job. So I knew what the organizer meant when he said that putting workers in craft unions in an auto plant was like trying to fit a round peg into a square hole. I remember how fascinated I was when he explained the shop steward system which the union set up in plants where they had members—one shop steward for every ten workers. (What a far cry from the shop steward system in the UAW today, where in all too many cases one shop steward is expected to serve scores of workers!) When the organizer told how the union had successfully settled grievances in such plants as Fisher Body, Lincoln, Packard, and Briggs, I thought of our dismal failure in the Continental cylinder department. I promptly joined the union and became a member of Local 127.

In 1919 the Auto Workers Union (AWU), as it was then called, struck the Wadsworth Body Company, which tried to break the union with Ford's help. The company imported strikebreakers and used the police, but production was cut drastically. The union might have won the strike if the plant had not burned down in August 1919. The plant was located near where I lived, and like scores of other people I watched the blaze, which lit up the sky for miles. After I was fired at Continental Motors I got a job at the Zenith Carburetor Company on Hart Avenue. I guess I was the only AWU member in the plant, and I can't recall that I recruited a single worker. I did not attend union meetings, but I did subscribe to the union paper. This was a lively publication which printed union news, advocated independent political action, and carried announcements of labor events, including the weekly forum conducted in the union hall Sunday afternoons. I went to every forum. The meetings were chaired by I. Paul Taylor, a Highland Park preacher. Among the speakers who made a deep impression on me were young Philip Randolph; James Cousins, who later became mayor of Detroit and who was mistakenly credited with dreaming up Ford's five-dollars-a-day policy; and prominent members of radical organizations such as the IWW, Socialist Party, and the Anarchist Society.

Every meeting was a thrilling session for me, especially during the question and answer period. No holds were barred, and some of the young radicals who took the floor often gave the guest speakers a hard time. There was a young Scottish seaman, extremely well-read (it seems seamen have plenty of time to read while on the high seas), who developed a knack for taking a speaker's points one by one, exposing fallacies and contradictions. It was at such a forum that I first became acquainted with Joe Brown (more about him later). He had a bitter floor argument with Larry Davidow, a lawyer who at that time was a member of the Socialist Party.

How I used to envy the young radicals for their ability to get up on their hind legs and give a good account of themselves in give-and-take discussion! Once I mustered enough nerve to ask a question. I raised my hand, and when the chairman recognized me I became so nervous and flustered that I could hardly get the words out of my mouth. I don't know what the question was, but I do know that I had no desire to repeat that painful experience in subsequent meetings. At one of the forum meetings I met I. Rab, who invited me to attend a class in "Wage Labor and Capital" which he was conducting on a weekday in the union building. I liked the way he handled the class, and at his urging I joined the Marxian Club, which called itself a companion group to the Socialist Party of Great Britain.

When the depression following World War I set in, Detroit was a beehive of radical activity. Splits occurred in the Socialist Party, with some of the former members flocking into the Communist Party and some forming new groups like the Proletarian University and the Marxian Club. Also making themselves heard in those days were the Socialist Labor Party, the Industrial Workers of the World, the Anarchists, and free-lance radicals too individualistic to fit into any group. Some groups conducted forums of their own, like the Proletarian University, which was formed by Al Renner, John Keracher, and Dennis Batt. Batt was a powerful speaker and I never missed an opportunity to hear him. The Proletarian University also sponsored classes and published a magazine, the *Proletarian*, copies of which can still be found in the University of Michigan Labor Archives. The Proletarian University developed factions and splits, and eventually Batt, Renner, and Keracher formed the Proletarian Party.

Entering College

I met Miss Haug, a retired school teacher, for the first time when she delivered a lecture on geology to a socialist audience. She offered to teach English to a group of Young Socialists, and I was one of them. Not one of us had completed grade school and we were hungry for more formal education. One day Miss Haug said to us: "Why don't you fellows work your way through college? A college education will equip you to make a better contribution to the radical movement." She offered to coach us in mathematics, English, and other studies so we could enter high school and go on to college. I am eternally indebted to Miss Haug. I will never forget the pains she took to help me in algebra, over which I labored and sweated until simultaneous quadratic equations oozed from my ears. How I faltered and stumbled when I read passages from *Macbeth* aloud!

Thanks to Miss Haug I enrolled in a high school which in the fall of

1921 was connected with the Michigan State Normal College, now Eastern Michigan University in Ypsilanti, Michigan. I took some high school and college courses at the same time. I had little money but I did not need much, for I earned my meals by working as a busboy in a restaurant. After years of factory work, life in that pleasant small college town was like living in Arcadia. I enjoyed my studies and liked the instructors; I can still remember some of their names: Professor Harvey in psychology, Professor Jefferson in geography (he had a national reputation), Professor Downing in English.

When my first college year ended, I returned to Detroit and promptly found a job at Cadillac Motor Company grinding cylinders. I saved my money and returned to school in the fall. During final exams at the close of the second semester I became very ill, so fatigued and listless and so utterly exhausted that I drank endless cups of strong coffee to keep going. When exams were completed, I consulted a local doctor. He said there was nothing to worry about: "You are run down, so just take it easy for a few days and you'll snap out of it." But I didn't snap out of it, instead I became steadily weaker. One morning I saw little specks of blood in my mucus. So I went back to the doctor. This time he diagnosed the trouble as a chest cold and gave me more pills. How different my life might have been if that doctor had ordered a chest x-ray! But he didn't, not even when I saw him for the third time and reported I was losing weight.

When I returned to Detroit I did not have sense enough to go to a good hospital for a thorough checkup. Instead I followed a pattern I was to continue all during the rest of the 1920s: I got a job in a factory, worked until fatigue overtook me, and then "took a few days off." Or I quit my job and did not look for another one until my money was running low.

Back to Work

I think it was in 1925 that the motor companies found a way to eliminate cylinder grinding; some ingenious engineer invented a honing system and one man could hone twelve cylinders in the time it used to take to grind one. I hired out as a honer in the Hupp Motor Company—and lasted one night. The honing machines were equipped with six spindles, like a multiple drill press. You honed all six cylinders at one time; the spindles fed the hones into the cylinder bores automatically while a steady fine kerosene spray kept the hones damp. The operator had to watch the job every second to see that the bores were honed to within one-thousandth of an inch of required size. It was piecework, and I toiled furiously to keep up with the other hone workers.

One out of every three blocks I took off my machine was rejected by the inspector, because it was either undersized or out-of-round. Every rejected block had to be put on the machine for rehoning. When the shift ended, my clothes were soaked with kerosene and I was so exhausted that when I sat down in the streetcar I fell into a deep sleep and the conductor had to wake me at the end of the line, far past my stop. Several days passed before I recovered from that ordeal. Then I looked for a job elsewhere.

Volumes have been written about the alienated factory worker, about speedup, about monotony and boredom of repetitive operations on the assembly line. I have read books on the subject by sociologists and industrial psychologists. From such studies I gained new theoretical insights, but they were pale compared to my gut memories of what it was like to be an auto production worker during the twenties. Picture the scene on a Baker streetcar when it was filled with Ford Rouge workers who came off the second shift around midnight: most of those lucky enough to get seats fell asleep almost as soon as they sat down. Many of those who had to stand fell asleep on their feet, swaying back and forth while holding car straps.

I remember what agonies of hell I suffered every time I worked the night shift. I couldn't sleep in the daytime; I couldn't eat; I always felt in a daze. Once I worked in the ring gear department of the General Motors Gear and Axle plant on Holbrook Avenue. It was a twelve-hour shift, from six in the evening until six in the morning, with a half hour off for lunch. The job was timed so that the operator had to work every minute in every hour, with no rest periods and no fatigue-time allowance whatsoever. I was running an internal grinder; every gear had to be ground to plug-gauge (a tool for measuring internal diameters) size. My right hand burned with raw blisters from forcing the gauge in the gears. We ate lunch in a large room supplied with benches. Like so many of the other workers, I gulped down a sandwich and a cup of coffee, then lay on the floor to sleep until the whistle called us back to work.

One night I had machine trouble and fell behind in production. The straw boss, a subhuman pusher who had the authority to hire and fire, bellowed like a bull. When I tried to explain that I had machine trouble, he roared: "I don't give a damn what you had, you get out production or you get fired—that's the rule around here, and no goddamn excuses!" I removed my shop apron, shut down my machine, bundled up my tools, punched out my timecard, and walked out of the plant. When I got to the gate the watchman told me that he could not let me out without a pass. I told him I had quit and wanted to go home. "If I let you through this gate without a pass I'll get fired, you know that," he told me. So I went back into the plant and asked the straw boss for a pass. "Pass my ass, you get no goddamn pass from me," he said. I told him flatly I would not work on the machine and he told me just as flatly that he would see me in hell before he would give me a pass. I went to the lunch room, curled up on a bench, and promptly fell asleep. But I did not sleep long. The straw boss came in and roared: "This ain't no hotel, no sleeping here!" Then I went to the toilet and sat on the stool until the whistle blew in the morning.

After that experience I made up my mind to quit production work forever and go into the tool room. I hired out as a tool grinder in a small tool and die plant on Fort Street. I was able to stick it out for about two weeks before the foreman told me I was too slow and he'd have to let me go. I worked in at least a dozen such small shops before I acquired enough competence to perform any grinding job in the tool room, whether external, internal, or surface grinding.

Reading Sprees

In those days the auto industry had its model-change layoff period in late summer. The workers referred to the layoff as their "starvation vacation." I don't know how the laid-off auto workers with families to support managed to live during those payless weeks. There was no unemployment compensation to tide them over until they returned to work. And when they did work they never earned more than enough to keep the family going from payday to payday.

Those were the days of the "suitcase brigade." When the auto companies were rushing like mad to get out production, they advertised for help in Tennessee, Kentucky, and Indiana. "Hillbillies" lugging cardboard suitcases traveled to Detroit by bus and got jobs on the assembly lines, leaving their families behind. Living in cheap rooming houses and eating in cheap restaurants, they managed to accumulate a stake by the time the model-change layoff season arrived; then they returned to their farms.

During changeover the industry would tool-up in preparation for the new models and tool and die shops worked overtime. I always refused to work overtime because the long hours were too much of a drain on my strength. The foreman cajoled and threatened to fire me, but I still refused, and he tolerated me because tool grinders were not easy to replace during tool-up season. Sometimes I worked only three days a week and spent the other days on Belle Isle Park reading. I can remember times when I took the streetcar to work in the morning, got as far as the factory gate, and then suddenly decided to spend the day on Belle Isle.

I had an incentive to read, not a material incentive, not a go-getter incentive, but of a different kind. The Marxian Club sponsored study classes, debates, and informal discussions. Morris Field, who later became an able union negotiator on the international UAW staff, conducted a class in economics, using *Das Kapital* as the text. I taught a class in "Socialism, Utopian and Scientific," and I spent hours preparing my lessons, especially the lessons pertaining to metaphysics and dialectics, the section which had once caused me such painful embarrassment. I went to the library and took out books that would facilitate my understanding of what Engels was driving at. Then I went to Belle Isle to "bone up" on the subject. There was a kind of intellectual rivalry among us in that club. Each tried to outshine the other. We spurned "bourgeois values" in terms of material status, but we had our own kind of snobbery. We considered ourselves well informed. So and so was said to be well informed about economics, another about history, another about literature, and some fancied themselves well informed about everything.

I used to go on reading sprees. For a while it was a Bertrand Russell spree, and I read book after book by Russell. Then it was a Karl Kautsky spree, and I read everything from his *Ethics* to his *Labor Revolution*. Sometimes I went for imaginative literature—plays by Shaw, Ibsen, O'Neill, novels by Dreiser, Anatole France, Tolstoy, and others.

Not far from our Marxian Club was Greenfield's Restaurant on Woodward Avenue. We spent hours there, discussing, arguing, pontificating over coffee or tea. Members of the Communist Party dubbed us "intellectual snobs" and referred to us as "tea drinkers" because there were a number of Englishmen in our group. Our opponents said we expected to achieve the revolution sitting in armchairs and drinking tea. We in turn called them apostles of dicta-torship, for they approved of everything the Russian Bolsheviks did.

I am reminded of the remark made by the steelworker whom Studs Terkel interviewed for a 1972 article in *Dissent*: "That's why it amazed me to find out, years ago—I read Jack London's 'Martin Eden'—can you imagine working people at a picnic discussing De Leon and Marx and all that? Today, forget it. I don't know what happened. I think what happened was the people who organized the working man forgot the spirit and paid more attention to the organization." Today you won't find young factory workers boning up on De Leon or Marx. Today the motivation is different; many young workers enroll in labor courses sponsored by university labor-relations institutes. None of these workers carries a thumb-worn copy of Herbert Spencer's *First Principles* in his pocket as did the young Welshman in our Marxian Club. Today they carry briefcases containing class materials on steward training, collective bargaining, or labor law. And their aim is not knowledge for its own sake, but training for union posts. We young radicals in the 1920s used to denounce "AFL piecards" (paid union officials). We had no way of knowing that our study class and soapbox experience would someday enable us to become piecards ourselves.

The old United Automobile, Aircraft, and Vehicle Workers of America (UAAVWA) succumbed to the postwar depression in the early twenties. Later the Communist Party (CP) picked up the pieces, formed the Auto Workers Union, and tried to direct it along industrial union lines. By that time I was firmly convinced that auto workers needed a union and I volunteered to help the CP in any way I could. I took a bundle of their leaflets into the shop and furtively placed them near the time clock so that each worker could take one when he punched his timecard. The leaflets explained the aims of the AWU and invited workers to come to a scheduled meeting.

Shop Papers

Some labor scholar would do well to write a research paper about the labor activities of the Communist Party in the auto centers during the twenties. What fresh and lively shop papers they put out! There were the *Hudson Worker*, the *Packard Worker*, the *Ford Worker*, and others. Those papers had the smell of machine oil about them. They fairly bristled with live, on-the-spot shop reports, exposing flagrant health hazards in the paint shop, describing brutal acts of this or that foreman toward the men under him, citing facts and figures about speedup on specific job operations, revealing how workers got shortchanged by a bonus system no one could ever figure out. Today most papers put out by UAW locals are usually filled with canned news about state and national politics, officers' reports, and petty shop gossip. Even lead stories about pending negotiations with the company over major grievances are generally written to enhance the prestige of local officers. Flagrant company violations of the union contract, excessive speedup, glaring health hazards in the factory—such news would reflect on the union local administration and so doesn't get printed.

The AWU shop papers were read eagerly by the workers. One day during lunch hour an AWU organizer set up a soapbox in front of the Hudson Motor Company and proceeded to give an organizational talk. He did not get an enthusiastic response. I was working at Hudson Motor at the time and I remember how workers, leaning out of windows, made snide remarks: "Hey, buddy, what's your racket?" "Why don't you make an honest living for a change?" "If you sounded off like that in Russia, they'd shoot you!"

The organizer spoke only about ten minutes, then handed out copies of the *Hudson Worker*. The headline featured the dubious bonus system then in effect at Hudson Motor. I listened to the comments: "By God, that's just how it is—you never can figure out how the hell much you are going to make by that bonus system. The harder you work the more you think you are going to earn and then when payday comes, the less you get!" They laughed gleefully about what the paper had to say concerning a certain foreman: "It's about time someone put out the dirt on that son of a bitch!"

The paper gave them a visceral reaction; it spoke to them about the experiences that impinged on their nerves, muscles, and brains. The paper said what they felt! How did the editors get their news "hot from the shops"? Did the CP have cells in the plant, people who worked in the various departments and reported their observations? Or did the AWU have contacts in the form of nonpolitical workers who belonged to the union and served as reporters? I don't know. But I do know that those papers played a significant role in preparing auto workers' minds for the union thrust that was to come in the days ahead.

In addition to exposing speedup, fraudulent incentive systems, and accident hazards, the shop papers publicized the employers' discriminatory practices: the way Negroes were confined to the dirtiest and meanest jobs, such as "bull work" in the foundry and clean-up work in toilets. I can credit those papers for making me conscious of the fact that Negroes have special problems as a minority group, apart from the general conditions of wage workers.

Up to that time I had a simple theory about the working class, a theory propagated by the Marxist sectarians with whom I was associated. The theory held that all those who work for wages are members of the working class and have the same interests regardless of race, creed, or nationality. The plight of any section of the working class, any minority, could only be solved when the entire working class became free of the yoke of wage slavery. We used to poke fun at the Communist Party line on the "Negro problem," especially the slogan: "self-determination for Negroes!" The Party called for a black republic within the United States—a demand as unworkable as it is unwise. Norman Thomas correctly characterized that CP demand as "a call for the worst kind of segregation."

But the CP opened my eyes to things about which I had been stone blind! I began to realize that black workers did have special problems. Because of discrimination they could not even get a hamburger in a cheap "greasy spoon" near the factory. They were never given a chance to break in on machines in the production department. And where they did work on the line, as in body shops like Briggs Manufacturing Company, they were relegated to dirty, damp, laborious work like wet sanding. Even on such jobs they were paid lower rates than whites received for comparable work.

Hard to Organize

Of all the radical groups active in the 1920s, the IWW and the CP were alone in the conviction that the auto industry could be organized along industrial union lines. I doubt that the Socialist Party (SP), the Proletarian Party (PP), or any of the lesser sects held any hope for effective unionism in the auto industry. The leaders of the Proletarian Party contended that the small portion of auto workers which could be organized would have to join the AFL; machine workers would have to join the machinist union; sheet metal workers would have to join the sheet metal workers union, and so on. The PP argued that industrial unionism was the only kind that made sense in the auto industry but it was not practical, and the PP advanced reasons as to why it could not be achieved. The work force was composed of so many different nationalities: Poles, Italians, English, Germans, Slavs, and many others, not to mention the "hillbillies," "sodbusters," and "crackers" from places like Kentucky, Tennessee, and Indiana—workers lured to Detroit factories by the "high wages." How could a work force composed of such dissimilar elements ever be brought together to tackle corporate giants like General Motors, Ford, and Chrysler?

When William Green, president of the AFL, wrote to the Automobile Manufacturers Association asking for a conference to weigh the pros and cons of unionism, the arrogant auto barons did not even deign to reply. They were determined to maintain an open shop industry, and to this end they employed industrial spies to ferret out any and all workers who "talked union." Past efforts to organize an industrial union in the auto industry failed dismally.

The old UAAVWA floundered and died and the AWU was getting nowhere—it was simply a paper union. In those days we all knew that "the AF of Hell" was not in the least interested in organizing a strong industrial union because such an organization would threaten the entrenched jobs of many craft union leaders. "How can auto workers be organized into a strong industrial union?"—I heard this proposition debated by Al Renner and a CP member, with Renner taking the negative side. I heard the same question thrashed out time and again by radicals in their meetings. I agreed with those who contended that the organizing attempts of the AWU would prove as futile as the labors of Sisyphus. Yet I believed that radicals should at all times advocate industrial unionism rather than craft unionism in the auto industry. This was my themesong at street meetings. Once when I climbed down from a soapbox an AWU organizer in the audience said: "When you argue with us you claim industrial unionism can't ever succeed in auto, but on the soapbox you advocate it as strongly as we do—just where in hell do you stand on this question?" I quoted a remark attributed to Debs: "You must work for what you believe in, even if you lose out in the end."

In those days the Communist International pursued its "Third Period" policies—and what crazy antics those policies called for! In America the CP declared war against the AFL and sought to win the membership away from the top-ranking leaders by calling for a "united front from below." The AFL leadership was castigated as "flunkies of the bosses," and the CP sought to organize dual unions in the coal, auto, textile, and other industries. I think they were most successful in textile areas of the south, where they conducted some bitter strikes. The CP leaders were utterly ruthless in their dealings with such rival organizations as the Proletarian Party, which professed to be the only sound communist organization in the United States. The CP never failed to use the double-cross tactic when it suited its purpose.

How well I remember what happened one evening in 1927 when a group of organizations held a mass meeting in Cadillac Square, demanding immediate freedom for Sacco and Vanzetti, who were slated for execution that night. Among organizations sponsoring the meeting were the central body of the AFL, the Communist Party, Proletarian Party, the Anarchists, and the Wobblies. The arrangements committee received permission from the police to hold the meeting, after pledging there would be no disturbance. A large crowd gathered and everything seemed to be going according to plan. I was one of the speakers and found myself addressing the largest audience I had ever faced in my life. Also speaking was Frank Martel, president of the AFL central body, and during his remarks he called on the workers to "join the union of your craft."

The most rousing speech was given by a fiery Italian anarchist, whose oratory brought the Italians in the crowd to a pitch of emotional frenzy. The CP speaker warned "the American ruling class" of the dire consequences that would follow in this land if Sacco and Vanzetti were killed. As the last speaker had his say and the chairman was about to close the meeting, the leader of the CP contingent gave a prearranged signal for action. The Party boys ran to a nearby truck, grabbed placards, and responded to the order: "On to the city hall!" The police, who had been positioned at strategic sections, quickly formed a cordon around city hall and the inevitable happened—confrontation between Communists and police.

Frank Martel lashed out at the CP leader who gave the order to march on city hall: "What's the matter with you damn fools? You gave your word that you would abide by the agreement with the police; now we'll pay hell before we ever get another permit to hold a street demonstration. And why in hell march on city hall? Do you bastards want to rape the scrubwomen over there?" But the Communists achieved their aim. Within a few hours the *Detroit Free Press* hit the streets with screaming headlines about the "riot." Said Martel: "Now the Party boys can send copies of the *Free Press* to Moscow to show they are on the job!"

Despite their "Third Period" absurdities, the Communists helped pave the way for industrial unionism. By speaking at factories and by distributing thousands of papers, leaflets, pamphlets, and other materials at shop gates, the Communists performed the kind of spadework that paid off when the CIO organizing drive got under way in the thirties. Though small in numbers, the AWU served as a training ground for workers who became shop-level leaders in later years.

Soapbox

To a lesser degree, organizations like the PP, IWW, SP, and such offshoots of the Communist Party as the Trotskyites and Lovestoneites afforded training for people who were destined to take active roles in building the UAW. The Proletarian Party (which I joined when the Marxian Club disbanded) held classes in public speaking as well as in labor history, economics, and, of course, the "socialist classics." Soapboxing in those days was an institution in Detroit, and some of the speakers became forceful orators. Every Saturday evening we held forth at Woodward and Temple streets; the opening speaker sounded off for fifteen minutes or so, to be followed by speaker after speaker. From practice the speakers learned how to use their voices effectively, how to parry questions, and how to handle hecklers. During the week we spoke on Detroit's East Side at Hillger and Jefferson streets and also at Hasting and Erskine streets.

During the twenties Hastings Street was still called "Kike Town" although the Jews were rapidly moving into better areas, and Hastings soon became part of the Black Belt. I don't know whether Jews or Negroes predominated in the area when we soapboxed there, but I remember that I had more success than the other speakers in holding the attention of Negroes in the audience—and for good reason. I belabored the auto companies for their racist hiring practices; I drew on endless examples of flagrant discrimination in the shop; and I asked such rhetorical questions as: Is there any reason why Negroes should not be promoted to cushion building? Is there any reason why they should be chained to the foundry or to mopping toilets? The Negroes responded to my questions in chorus: "He's right! He's right!"

I don't think I ever told my black audience that white workers were just as opposed to extending job promotion to Negroes as the employers were. I suspect my radical bias made me concentrate all my denunciation against "the bosses." But I knew only too well how filled with racial prejudice white workers were, especially white southerners. I knew that one of the foremen I worked under in Timken Axle was an active Klansman. The Klan was strong in eastern Michigan in those days. The workers in my department were sympathetic to the Klan: "The Klan keeps communists and niggers in their place!" It would be interesting to know how many southerners who worked in the plants then actually belonged to the Klan and donned white robes and met in secret places at night.

In January 1929 I got a job tool grinding in the Detroit Lubricator Company on Trumbull Avenue. In that year "prosperity" reached its peak, yet there was so much unemployment in Detroit that the *Free Press* carried pictures of job seekers massed at the employment offices of the Ford Motor Company. I was still single and still working three days a week, just long enough to earn board and room and incidental expenses. I had no car, not even a cheap jalopy, and I didn't want one, for I believed that the more material things I possessed and the longer I had to work to pay for them, the less free time I would have to spend at the library reading. This was how I spent most of my free time, but some days I hung around the AWU hall and discussed union organizing strategy and tactics with the organizers. There I sometimes got into heated arguments about the Russian Revolution; they quoted Lenin and Stalin and I quoted Kautsky and Luxemburg. Occasionally I went to the IWW hall and discussed the One Big Union with Wobblies.

I always got along amicably with the Wobblies, even though we disagreed on basic theory. Unlike CP members, the Wobblies treated opponents as opponents and not as enemies. To the CP, all other radical parties and groups were social fascists and therefore counterrevolutionists.

All radical outfits addressed themselves to "the American working class" but in those days the great bulk of the American workers were not even union conscious, much less class conscious. They did not discuss socialism when they held their bull sessions during lunch period, but a considerable number of them did talk about the stock market, what stocks they bought and how those stocks were rising week by week. It never occurred to them that "prosperity" would not continue forever. How they used to laugh at me when I predicted a depression! We radicals knew that a depression was on the way, but none of us thought it would come so soon or be so severe and last so long.

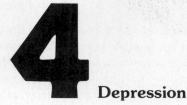

4 Depression

When the stock market crash rocked Wall Street in the fall of 1929, layoffs in the auto industry were not long in coming. There was much unemployment and suffering in Detroit that winter. In March 1930 the Communists organized a "hunger march" in many cities, including Detroit. In that city, people responded to the call by the thousands. Downtown Detroit was so jam-packed with people that some of the large plate glass windows in big department stores were pushed in. Mounted police ordered the crowd back, but there was no place to move, so the cops used their clubs on heads and shoulders. Never before nor since in this country were the Communists so successful when "calling the masses into the streets."

The huge turnout indicated how serious economic conditions were in that city only five months after the stock market collapsed. By 1931 Detroit, a one-industry town, was so paralyzed that it became known as "The City of the Dead." Nearly all of my friends and relatives were unemployed in the spring of 1930, and most of them were not to find jobs again for several years. The Detroit Lubricator plant slackened to a three-day week, and that suited me perfectly. I spent most of my spare time in radical activity—soapboxing, attending Marxist study classes, and passing out shop papers for the AWU. The papers exposed the way in which the employers were taking advantage of the depression to cut wages and increase speedup.

I think it was in June 1930 that the Lubricator plant laid me off. For about two weeks I looked for work, but I finally gave up the search, realizing it was futile. Most employment offices had "no help wanted" signs, and where there was no such sign the employment agent had a stock answer: "We're not hiring today." I knew there were many more jobbing shops and parts plants in Cleveland than in Detroit, so I decided to try my luck in that city. As in Detroit, so in Cleveland: looking for a job was an exercise in futility. During the day I looked for work and in the evening I became a "free-lance soapboxer."

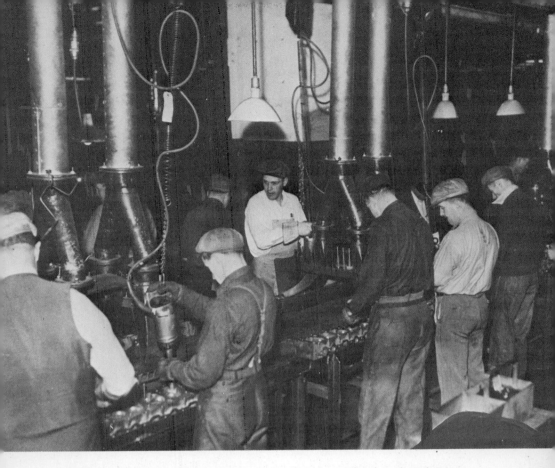

By the 1930s the assembly line technique had been developed to the point where cars could be assembled as fast as the men could work.

Cleveland had a free speech tradition that went back to the days of its famous liberal mayor, Tom Johnson. The large downtown square was available to any group, party, or individual seeking an audience. I spoke for short periods, called for questions, and then took up a collection. In this way I was able to supplement what little money I still had left. I lived in cheap rooming houses and ate in the cheapest restaurant, and with each passing day my savings dwindled. What to do? When a man has no money and can't find a job, he either becomes a bum and vegetates in one place or becomes a hobo and moves on. I knew there was a large General Motors plant as well as smaller parts plants in Buffalo, New York. So I went to the Nickel Plate Railroad, caught a freight train, and headed for that city.

Hoboing

Every employment office I went to in Buffalo was filled with job seekers, but of course no one was ever hired. When a man is unemployed and broke, he grasps for straws. When someone in Buffalo told me that a machine shop in Corning, New York, needed tool grinders, I lost no time getting to the Erie Railroad and catching a freight train going east. Every Erie freight train was loaded with hoboes in those days. They rode in empty boxcars, on top of boxcars, in gondolas, on the running boards of oil tankers, and on flat cars. Some of them, like myself, rode in hopes of eventually finding a job; others rode for the sheer sake of traveling. As one hobo told me, "When you know damn well you can't find a job, it's a hell of a lot better to ride the rods than to sit home brooding." It was amusing to hear those who had been east warn their "fellow passengers": "For Christ's sakes, don't go east; you can't buy a job anywhere in that part of the country!" And those who came from the west or midwest gave the same dire warning about those regions. I soon discovered that hoboing was not the romantic experience depicted in Jack London's *The Road*. There is nothing romantic about sleeping in public parks, police stations, and in boxcars. And knocking on back doors, offering to do chores in return for something to eat, is not exactly a dignified way to make a living. I preferred asking a storekeeper for a can of pork and beans, a loaf of day-old bread, and a little loose coffee. Then I went to the nearest hobo jungle, made coffee in a tin can, hollowed out the loaf of bread, and filled it with the pork and beans.

I did not find work in Corning or in any other town along the Erie Railroad in New York and New Jersey. Several times when riding freights through farmland I got off and applied for work as a farmhand. A farmer eager to have his hay off the ground and into the barn before the rain came would hire me. Pitching hay all day would just about do me in! The farmer paid me two dollars a day plus room and board. The room was a hayloft and the board consisted of bread and potatoes.

One farm I worked on was operated by Harry Miles, who once owned the farm but was now running it on a crop-sharing basis for the bank that took it over in lieu of mortgage payments. Poor Miles! Living with him were his two daughters, one the mother of an illegitimate child

The apple stand came to be the depression trade mark.

and the other a divorcee who had custody of her two-year-old daughter. The two sisters fought like snarling cats. I can still hear Minnie's shrill cry: "Damn you, Helen, you and your brat ain't gonna sleep in MY bed anymore. Buy your own damn bed!" And Miles would plead: "Now, now, Minnie, that ain't a way to talk to your sister. . . ." I witnessed rural poverty at its worst. Miles, his daughters, and their children lived on potatoes and green vegetables—no milk, no meat, no cheese ever. I doubt if they knew what the word "protein" meant.

I liked Miles; he was a kindly man, but a terribly defeated man. I was anything but a "handyman" around his farm, and he observed my awkward work movements with amused tolerance. "Hell's fire man, you ain't ever gonna be a farmer. You can't even learn to hold a pitchfork right!" Miles just couldn't comprehend how he and so many others lost their farms. In the simplest terms I tried to explain the reasons for the depression, and especially the reasons for the plight of the American small farmers. But I could never get through to him. Over and over he asked: "Do you think the automobile ruined the farmer?" I could never get that strange fixation out of his head. For some reason I could never fathom, he seemed firmly convinced that the automobile was the demon that ruined him.

After two weeks of pitching hay, hoeing corn, and subsisting on a poor diet, I bade Miles and his daughters goodby and caught an Erie freight train heading west. I rode to Syracuse and spent several days there tramping for work. I was like the work-stiff the Wobblies sang about: "Tramp, tramp, keep on a tramping, there's nothing doing here for you!" I knew that the Proletarian Party had a branch in Rochester, so one afternoon I climbed up on the tender of a New York Central passenger train and rode into that city. I contacted members of the Proletarian Party, and one of them offered to let me stay in his home until I landed a job.

Although Rochester had many diversified industries, factory jobs were not to be had. Western New York is famous for its rich fruit belt, and I arrived in Rochester at a time when farmers needed pickers. I don't remember how much I received for each basket of peaches, pears, and apples I picked, but while the season lasted I earned enough to pay for my room and board. When the harvest season ended, I picked up odd jobs. For a while I tried selling vacuum cleaners from house to house, but I soon learned that housewives were not about to spend money on durable goods like vacuum cleaners when a broom would do. So I peddled brooms—floor brooms, whisk brooms, brushes. I bought my wares from the broom factory at wholesale price and sold them at retail price. I looked upon every housewife who came to the door as either a prospective customer or a prospective employer. If she did not need a broom or a brush I asked if she needed something done around the house—a tree chopped down, perhaps, or the yard cleaned up, or whatever. In this way I was able to earn a few extra dollars.

In the winter of 1930–31 I was lucky enough to find a job waiting on tables in the Rathskeller of the Rochester Labor Lyceum. During the prohibition era the Rathskeller was frequented by Germans every Saturday night; they came to eat German food, dance to German music, and drink good German near-beer. I worked strictly for tips and was able to earn enough on Saturday night to pay for my room and for the food I bought and cooked during the week.

Rochester has always been noted for its cultural activities—the Eastman School of Music, a fine symphony orchestra, and an excellent library. I spent my days during the winter browsing in the library, where it was warm and clean and light and quiet. I did not study systematically but read at random: newspapers, magazines, fiction, history. The library was my place of escape; reading kept me from brooding over the insecurity of prolonged unemployment. The Proletarian Party conducted classes in the Labor Lyceum two evenings of each week. The text used in one of those classes was *The Origin of the Family, Private Property, and the State* by Friedrich Engels. To prepare for this class, I spent hours reading up on the various family forms and marriage customs of different historical periods.

How seriously we took ourselves in that small sectarian outfit called the Proletarian Party! We were only a vestpocket study group, yet we boasted of being a sound revolutionary party—and, of course, we had all the correct answers. We used to discuss current events and always ended up by taking a "position" on every important event of the time. We endorsed and rationalized about every twist and turn of the Third International, while at the same time criticizing the American Communist Party for carrying out the policies dictated by that International. And as for Stalin's genocidal policies toward the Russian peasantry, we contended that the capitalist press greatly exaggerated the mass starvation resulting from those policies, and we insisted that the only victims were the rich peasants, the "kulaks" who sabotaged socialist agrarian reconstruction and therefore received the punishment they deserved.

We prided ourselves on being the only true revolutionary party in America. We knew our theories were right because they were grounded on the Marxist-Leninist principles of the class struggle, historical materialism, and the "law of value." Thanks to the law of value, capitalism was floundering in a catastrophic depression from which it could never recover; consequently, all measures adopted by government and business to save the economic system were doomed to failure. Increasing misery would descend on the masses, who would rise up in violent revolution, which we, the vanguard, would lead and direct into the dictatorship of the proletariat. Like a religious sect waiting for the Second Coming, we were certain the revolution would come in our time.

Kitchen Hand

One day in the spring of 1931, Cy Ware, a member of the Proletarian Party who worked as a waiter in Iola Tuberculosis Sanatorium in Rochester, told me the head chef needed another kitchen hand. He warned: "The work will be hard—Oscar, the chef, drives himself hard and drives his help even harder." I immediately applied for the job and was lucky enough to get hired at thirty dollars a month "and all the food you can eat." The work was hard. My job called for helping the first cook, which meant that I had to lift heavy pots and pans of food, mop the floor, carry kettles to the dishwasher, lift crates of vegetables and large boxes of meat—all the chores that are expected of a cook's helper in a large institution.

Kitchen hands got one day off a month. We worked from six in the morning until one in the afternoon, got two hours off, and then worked again from three to six in the evening. I was not used to working that hard and that steady. I always felt tired and literally "ran on my nerves," consuming endless cups of coffee and chain-smoking cigarettes. The produce scale in the storeroom showed me that I was losing weight, yet it never occurred to me that there might be something organically wrong. I spent my precious "free day" at the beach, not realizing that lying in the sun was the worst thing I could have done, in view of what was ailing me.

After I had worked in Iola about three months, Oscar called the kitchen staff together and informed us that Dr. Bridge, the superintendent, ordered all kitchen hands to have an x-ray taken "as a precautionary measure." I recall arguing with Oscar about this: "It's silly for us to get a chest x-ray. How could I ever heave those heavy kettles of soup bones on the stove if I had tuberculosis?" Oscar said orders were orders and "if Dr. Bridge orders an x-ray you better damn well get an x-ray!" I even told the x-ray technician she was wasting her time "taking my picture." "I might be skinny but that's no sign I have TB," I assured her. "You can never tell until you get this kind of a checkup," she said.

The next morning I heard the bad news. I still recall the sickening sensation in my stomach as I listened to Dr. Bridge's report: "You have a small cavity in your right lung. The scar tissue on your lung indicates that you have had TB on and off over the years, but apparently you had enough resistance to hold the disease in check in that area." When I asked him how serious my condition was and how long I might have to "take the cure" his answer was succinct: "There is no way of knowing; all we can tell you is that time and rest—yes, time and rest—will eventually cure you."

Death in the Family

Fate wasn't kind to the Marquart brothers that summer. About ten days after my status in Iola changed from kitchen hand to hospital patient, my sister in Detroit informed me by telegram that my brother Bill died. While attending a swimming party with friends in Canada, Bill broke his neck when he dove off a pier into shallow water. He was rushed to a Canadian hospital and died a few weeks later.

Upon receiving the bad news I wrote the following letter to my sister:

August 19, 1931

Dear Betty,

You can imagine how I felt when I received your telegram reporting Bill's death. In a way I'm glad my illness precludes my going to Detroit for the funeral. I want to remember Bill as I last saw him in life and not as a corpse mummified by the mortician's art. I remember so well when Bill was born. It was a bitterly cold day in February 1908. On that blizzardy morning the old man made me fetch a bucket of water from the well, which was about 200 yards from our house, while he stayed in the warm kitchen. But that was in keeping with Big Nick's character. So many painful memories stick out in my mind about our unhappy childhood when we lived in that old log cabin in Braddock Hills. I recall the evening when our parents had one of their all-too-frequent violent quarrels. Bill was still a tot in arms and you were five years old. Suddenly the old man was seized by one of his furious rages. He grabbed a bucket of cold water which I had just brought from the well and poured it over Mother. And that other fight when he pushed her against the wall and began choking her until she started to get blue in the face! We three kids screamed in terror. You threw your little arms around his leg and pleaded: "Please don't kill my Mother." This brought him to his senses; he picked you up in his arms and tried to calm you.

I remember that small farm, those ten acres of fertile land. I'll say this about the old man: he certainly had a green thumb; he knew how to make things grow. And he had two slaves that he put to work on that land—Mother and me. We had to spade, weed, hoe, harvest the vegetables and prepare them for market. I became a huckster at the age of seven. Summertime was no vacation from school for me. Every day, six days a week, I would carry two baskets loaded with lettuce, onions, spinach, green beans, tomatoes, and anything else we could grow. For five successive summers I lugged baskets those three miles to Swissvale, and peddled vegetables from house to house. In those days I was so skinny that the school kids named me "beanpole."

The baskets were too heavy for me. By the time I was twelve years old I already had round shoulders and curvature of the spine. On the average I would sell $1.50 worth of vegetables, some days more, some days less. The more money I brought home the more booze the old man could buy in the saloons of Braddock and East Pittsburgh. Sunday after Sunday he would go to his German Club in East Pittsburgh to drink and have a good time with his friends. Not once—not one single time—did he ever take Mother with him, though most men in that club brought their wives. To him Mother was not a human being; she was his work beast, and so was I. Fortunately you and Bill were too young to be turned into farm hands and hucksters. But your lives were no beds of roses either. At least I was not thrown into an orphanage, the way he dumped you and Bill into what you once called "that snake pit of a Catholic Home" in Pittsburgh. When the family broke up that time, he claimed he was too poor to pay room and board to a private family for the two of you. But I know that he spent more money in saloons than it would have cost him to board his two kids. You and I know that his nightmarish experience in that orphanage did incredible harm to Bill's emotional life.

One thing always puzzled me: What was it that made Old Nick hate Bill so much? To be sure, he was mean to all of us, to Mother and me and you—although not quite as much to you because you were his "little girl." But he was positively fiendish to Bill. Why? There was something eating him about Bill that we don't know about. He never beat Bill physically but you know how he went out of his way to harass him, to browbeat him, to curse and bully him. Bill would become terrified when he had to work with the old man, like cleaning up the yard or fixing something in the basement or in the tool shed, or whatever. You know how nervous Bill always was; his fingers trembled worse than a very old man's. As I look back I think Nick derived a sadistic delight in torturing Bill, in downgrading him, in making him feel unwanted, in crippling his ego. He made Bill feel horribly insecure. Once, when he was about eighteen, Bill asked me: "Do you think life is worth living?" I pooh-poohed his question, told him not to talk like a damn fool, that he had a long life of adventure and fun ahead of him. More than once I heard him bring up that subject in different words. Bill was a good swimmer and a good diver. Over and over I ask myself: "Why that recklessness of diving off that pier without first investigating the depth of the water???"

When the Briggs Harper plant fire occurred in 1927 I jokingly told Bill his guardian angel hovered over him and he was doomed to live to be 100 years old. He had a lucky escape. The fire was on a Saturday morning and started in the department where Bill was employed. That old fire trap of a Harper plant was filled with ignitable paint and fumes and in no time the fire engulfed whole sections of the plant. I forget how many workers burned to death, in addition to the thirty men and women who left their homes to go to work (and persons saw them at their work benches) but none of whom returned home or have been seen since. The Briggs management denied having any record to show they reported to work that day, and therefore the company could not be held liable. I also know that Briggs's high officials went around the day after the fire and sought to settle liability of the company by paying $100 each to the families of the victims officially reported killed. Imagine, $100 for a life! My God, Betty, when will the auto slaves wake up and organize a strong union! Well, on that Saturday morning Bill felt indisposed and did not report for work! He called it a "lucky hunch." Little did I think that only four years later. . . .

Bill is gone. In 1928 Mother died (I writhed inside when I saw the old man shed crocodile tears at her grave). I'm in this sanatorium—for how long no one can say. Your husband's business, like thousands of other small businesses, got shattered by the depression. But your big consolation is that you have three fine children. And as for the old man, well, ever since he started to work in Stanley's blind pig [a place where alcoholic drinks were served during prohibition] in 1924, he's been in heaven. He loves to tend bar, he eats well and can swill all the booze he desires.

I know how close you and Bill always were, and his death must be a severe blow to you. When the funeral is over, you should take a trip. Why don't you plan to take the boat to Buffalo and then come to Rochester to visit me? From here you can go to Cleveland, where I know you have fond friends.

Affectionately,
Frank

P.S. I don't know if you are aware that I tried again and again to interest Bill in socialism, but in vain. Why did I become a radical and not Bill? God knows he had every reason to rebel against something! He didn't even rebel against the old man. Once he told me, "Really, I don't hold any ill will against Pa." I looked at him in disbelief!

Leisure

Now I was a convalescent. No longer did I have to heave heavy kettles, mop the floor, and perform all the hard work of a kitchen hand. I took to my new life like a duck to water. No economic worries for me now! Now

I had hearty meals, a comfortable bed, and endless hours of leisure for reading whatever the mood dictated. In his *Summing Up* Somerset Maugham tells about his brief bout with TB and how he spent his convalescence reading scores of books. I never kept a record of all the books I read during my stay in Iola (we called it the "San"), but there were many—novels, histories, plays, and, of course, radical literature. I had an inspiration to read. Mary MacCollum, a member of the Proletarian Party, came to visit me three times each week. She was eager to learn about Marxism, and I was only too happy to act as her teacher. She insisted that we tackle the first volume of Marx's *Kapital*. "You translate the chapters into understandable language and mail a lesson to me every day," she ordered. She provided me with a second-hand portable typewriter and a manual for learning the touch system. Every morning I sat propped in bed, practicing the touch system. In time I mastered the keyboard but my rhythm stuttered (and still does). Mary, an office secretary, kept me supplied with plenty of typing paper and carbon sheets.

And so began a long and delightful teacher-student relationship. Patients were permitted to "go home" one day each month. How eagerly I looked forward to spending my free day with Mary in her apartment. We discussed "our lessons," dreamed up plans for our future, and acted on Bertrand Russell's advice concerning innocent pleasure.

Months passed, but the disease showed no signs of yielding to the cure; every sputum test turned out to be positive. Today, thanks to the latest discoveries of medical science, TB patients can be cured in a matter of months. But in those days there were no magic drugs for speeding up recovery from TB. What seems so awful to me when I look back is the fact that I actually did not want to get cured! I always sighed with relief when I learned that the sputum test was still positive. In those terrible days of economic depression I dreaded the thought of leaving the San and struggling for a livelihood. I knew I could never again do heavy physical work or return to tool grinding and breathing emery dust. I saw what happened to some of my fellow patients when they were cured and left the San to battle the job market. Some had to take jobs that were too strenuous for them and in time they had relapses and had to return to the San. I knew others who "broke down" due to the stress and strain of the long and futile search for work.

No, I didn't want to leave the San. I wanted no part of the

depression misery on the outside. Friends in Detroit wrote to me about the miseries in that city. Joe Brown, then a Federated Press (a labor news service) correspondent, wrote authentic reports about men lining up at night behind the big hotels waiting for the garbage cans to be brought out. Joe incurred the wrath of some city officials with his story of the young woman who collapsed in Grand Circus Park and died before the ambulance got to the hospital. Doctors pronounced her death due to starvation. Joe sent me snapshots of "Hoover shanties" erected from cardboard and tarpaper by poverty-stricken depression victims. In one of his letters, Joe wrote: "You don't know how lucky you are—you get three squares a day and have a good roof over your head."

For the first year I was content, even happy, to live the life of a convalescent. Then something happened that changed my mind and made me yearn for a fast recovery. One night I woke up hemorrhaging from my infected lung. (Patients called it "throwing a ruby.") I was immediately removed from the Pavilion, where patients had walking privileges, to the infirmary for complete bed rest. I won't attempt to describe the traumatic effect produced by a lung hemorrhage. I have seen patients go stir crazy soon after hemorrhaging. That did not happen to me. What worried me most was that a strict bed patient was deprived of his free day and that meant no visit to Mary's apartment. I took her advice: "Sure, it's tough. But don't let it get you down. We can make up for lost time later. Remember that peace of mind is the best healing agent. You keep sending me lessons, and I'll keep visiting you three times a week."

And so month followed month and every day I wrote a "lesson" for Mary. Sometimes it was an outline of a book, sometimes a review of a novel, sometimes a long comment on a *New York Times* feature article. Once I wrote a rather long letter to *The New York Times*, criticizing Father Coughlin's proposal to change from a gold standard to a silver standard. I spent hours working on that letter and more hours pruning what I wrote. I was delighted to see it published under a prominent headline in the Sunday issue of the *Times*. A staff doctor read it and suggested: "Why don't you try to break into the writing game professionally?" Unfortunately, I paid no attention to his suggestion.

Joe Brown

As a reporter for the Federated Press, Joe Brown kept scrapbooks of strike stories culled from Detroit dailies. In time his scrapbooks became known as the Joe Brown Collection and are now available to labor scholars in the Wayne State University Labor Archives. When a Wayne State professor heard that I knew Joe Brown personally he asked, "What sort of man was he?" Joe was a sheet metal worker and became a socialist when still an apprentice in Philadelphia, his home town. Later he came to Detroit, and I first met him when he joined our Marxian Club. Joe and I became fast friends over the years. In 1929 we shared an apartment on Peterboro Street near Cass Avenue. Joe was a member of the AFL Sheet Metal Workers Union and the recording secretary of his union local for many years. Joe and I often soapboxed at the same street corners. Religion was Joe's bugbear. He could reel off con-tradictions in the bible by the hour. He had a devilish sense of humor and could always draw a larger crowd than I could. He told his audience that he was a disciple of Karl Marx and Bob Ingersoll, and he alternated between "exposing" religion and explaining capitalist economics—"how the system really works." If his audience found his economic talk uninteresting or boring and began to drift away, Joe quickly switched to religion and told why men of the cloth chase after women a la Elmer Gantry: "They don't work; they eat well; they have excess energy; and they have to get rid of it somehow." Joe was at his best when handling hecklers, especially members of the Communist Party who accused him of being a Social Democratic reformer. Joe calmly pulled a copy of the *Communist Daily Worker* from his pocket and read off the reform measures advocated by the Party. He enjoyed the challenge of heckling, and his audience relished his repartee.

Joe was not a bookworm socialist, but an activist. During the twenties he was active in his own union and devoted much of his spare time to the Auto Workers Union. "I know the leaders of the AWU are Communists. I disagree with their philosophy and their politics, but when they try to organize the auto workers I'm with them," he once told me. Then he added, "The AF of Hell is not interested in organizing mass production workers so we must give a hand to those who are trying to organize them." During the depression Joe was jobless and broke for a long time. He ate in the "soup kitchen" set up by the IWW in Detroit, and he earned a few dollars now and then by sending stories to the Federated Press, said to be Communist controlled, but which reported organizing activities and strikes in industrial centers like Detroit.

By sending me Federated Press galleys, Detroit newspaper

clippings, and long letters, Joe kept me posted about labor events in the Motor City. In my files I have a Federated Press story (dated 19 September 1931) headlined: "Four Starve Daily in Detroit." The subhead reads: "200,000 have no jobs." And the lead paragraph: "A physician in the Receiving Hospital in Detroit told Federated Press recently that four people a day on the average are brought to the hospital too far gone from starvation for their lives to be saved."

Mass suffering in Detroit reached its highest pitch in 1932. In the spring of that year the Communists organized a march from Detroit to the huge Rouge Ford plant in Dearborn. The Federated Press reported the story: "On Monday, March 7, the Ford Motor Company has given an answer to the immediate needs of the employed and unemployed workers. The bloody attack against the 5000 hungry workers who began to march orderly for work or bread were met by Henry and Edsel Ford and supported by the Detroit and Dearborn police with tear gas, revolvers and machine gun fire. As a result of the savage attack four workers are dead and scores are wounded; many of them will be crippled for life."

Later the Federated Press reported the aftermath: "Ten thousand workers voiced their mighty protest at the Arena Gardens, ten thousand passed in endless lines by the biers of the four murdered men, seventy thousand marched with grim determination down Woodward Avenue behind the martyrs' coffins, twenty thousand stood at the cemetery, scores of thousands attended protest meetings throughout the country."

Joe was also active in an unemployed council in Detroit and was a member of the delegation elected to call on the Mayor and the city welfare department with specific demands for aid to the needy in the form of money, clothes, food, and coal. He was on the food committee which visited stores in the neighborhood to collect food and clothing. He once told me how he and other unemployed council members moved furniture back in the house of an evicted family after the sheriff and his men had carried the furniture out on the sidewalk. Knowing Joe, I could well imagine with what glee he helped to pressure city bureaucrats and thwart sheriffs on behalf of the poor.

The depression hit bottom in the winter of 1932 and employment picked up somewhat by January 1933, so the big motor companies and parts plants began to call back workers. If Marx's theory of increasing proletarian misery ever had any relevance it surely did that winter in

Detroit. With hundreds of workers desperately seeking jobs, the employers beat down wages and speeded up workers to the breaking point. That's when the wage slaves revolted. Letters I received from Brown made me itch for the day when I could return to Detroit. One letter said: "All hell is breaking out in this city now. Every day one hears how workers in some department throw down their tools and walk out when the bosses spurn their grievances. Bower Roller Bearing, Briggs, Packard—in plant after plant, strike fever is spreading and the workers are becoming more militant." Joe kept me posted on the developments of the Briggs strike. I had worked in the Briggs body shop and knew some of the men on the strike committee. I wrote to Joe: "How I wish I could fly to Detroit and walk in the picket line. Why, why, why do I have to be cooped up in this damn San at a time like this?" Here is Joe's version of what happened.   •

Briggs Strike

On 23 January 1933 the metal finishers in the Briggs Highland Park plant walked off their jobs when the company refused to consider their demands for a basic minimum wage rate of fifty-two cents an hour, a reduction in the speed of work, and the end of dead time (time for which workers were not paid when they reported for work and then had to wait sometimes for hours until the foreman could find work for them to do). The next day workers at the Briggs Detroit Mack Avenue plant joined the strike. Soon all the Briggs plants were closed down. "Don't deal with the strike committee or you'll get no more orders for bodies," the Automobile Manufacturers Association told Briggs. George Blackwood in his doctoral thesis on the history of the UAW summed up the course of the strike as follows:

Seeing the strike spread through its plants, the Briggs corporation used its great power to break the sudden uprising. It refused to deal with the strikers, charging Communist control, and stated proudly that it had never paid less than twenty-five cents an hour—although the picketers maintained that some of them had received less than ten cents an hour on the complicated piecework system. The strike dragged on for over two months, dying out after minor gains. The barely-organized group fell apart, with adherents of the Communist Party, the Proletarian Party, the Socialist Party, the Industrial Workers of the World and several other splinter groups working for control. The daily newspapers attacked the strike as "Red-inspired." Finally, Briggs

The Briggs strike of 1933. This strike, in which the Auto Workers took part, was one of the first major strikes of the 1930s.

imported strikebreakers through such agencies as Pinkerton, according to strikers.

The Briggs strike and the general labor unrest that smoldered during the summer of 1933 brought the AFL into the picture. The Federation decided to organize auto workers into federal locals, but skilled workers were to be kept out. The federal unions were to be called the United Automobile Workers; they were not to be given autonomy but administered by AFL appointees. Meanwhile the small, Communist-controlled Auto Workers Union called a convention in June to formulate ways and means to spur their organizational drive among auto workers. And then a third union appeared on the scene: the Mechanics Educational Society of America (MESA), composed mostly of skilled workers and headed by the irrepressible Matthew (Matt) Smith, who had been an active unionist in England.

Socialist, atheist, and iconoclast, Matt refused to become a citizen of the United States on principle: "I'm an internationalist, a citizen of the human race." Smith spurned the theory that employers are entitled to a profit: "The union's task is not to temper wage slavery—its ultimate goal is to function in a planned society as a national instrument of production, cooperating with a recast distributive system to make a Brave New World." He said the MESA must act as a revolutionary industrial organization which sets its sights on the common ownership of the means of production. He called the government labor boards set up under the National Industrial Recovery Act (NIRA) "sops to labor which actually work in the interest of the employers." But he did not hesitate to lay his revolutionary theories aside and use the labor board machinery when employers discriminated against the MESA.

By August 1933 the MESA claimed a membership of 5,000 in Detroit plus members in Flint and Pontiac. To the dismay of the AFL's International Association of Machinists, highly skilled tool and die makers turned to the more militant MESA, which offered membership without initiation fee and dues at 25¢ a month, compared to the IAM initiation fee of $5 and monthly dues of $1.75. In September 1933 the MESA waged the most widespread strike ever recorded in the auto industry up to that time. The strike started in the tool and die department of General Motors plants in Flint and then extended to Detroit, where it affected most of the main plants (except Ford), sixty-seven job shops associated with the Automotive Tool and Die Manufacturers Association, and sixty independent plants. The employers hoped to defeat the strike by announcing publicly that workers were returning to their jobs in droves, and they accused the MESA of using goon tactics to terrorize workers who wanted to go to work.

The companies also tried to frighten workers back to their jobs by threatening to move operations away from Detroit. When John Carmody, a member of the National Labor Board, came to Detroit to conciliate the strike he found that the employers resorted to stalling tactics rather than bargaining in good faith. The automobile manufacturers sat at the bargaining table with union representatives and discussed working conditions, but they made no attempt to arrive at a workable agreement. In other words, they blandly ignored the requirements of section 7(a) of the NIRA.

In some plants workers began to trickle back to work and for a while it appeared as if the strike might fail. It was then that the left-wingers in the MESA accused Smith and other leaders of failing to form a rank and file committee, of refusing to permit members of a Communist-led unemployed council to reinforce the picket line, and of not calling out the production workers. When the strike failed to stop automobile production, the left-wingers were given their chance, but their attempts to persuade semiskilled and unskilled production workers to join the strikers failed utterly.

Direct Action

As the days dragged on and the union was unable to effect a successful settlement, the strikers took things in their own hands. Joe Brown was an eyewitness to what happened:

People who say skilled workers are more conservative than production workers don't know what they are talking about. It's the skilled workers who are putting unionism on the map in Detroit. And they are using militant means to do it. October 30, 1933 will go down as a memorable day in the labor history of Detroit. I saw over 4000 workers form caravans of cars, and I was in one of those cars. We were out to do a job on the job shops. The route was laid out in advance. When we reached the first shop on the route we piled out of the cars, smashed all the windows, broke in the doors, burned blueprints, tore up expensive tool diagrams and smashed fixtures. Then we ran back to the cars and headed out for the next shop. Man, was that ever an exciting experience! We called it "educating the bosses." By the time the police got to the first shop we were already at the second one—always a stretch ahead of the cops. We started out around 9 in the morning and did not finish till past 4 in the afternoon. I think the cops finally caught up with some guys and arrested them, but I don't know how many. The capitalist press called our missionary work "vandalism" and accused the MESA leadership of instigating it. Hell, Matt Smith and the other MESA leaders couldn't have stopped it even if they had wanted to. The strikers are fed up to the gills with the anti-union shenanigans of the manufacturers—so they set out to teach them a lesson. And by God they taught them a lesson they won't forget in a hurry!

Such direct action brought results. Within two weeks the union reached a settlement with the companies affected; wages were to be increased five cents an hour, and there was to be no discrimination against strikers on rehire. Smith claimed that for all practical purposes the MESA obtained recognition in the jobbing shops. And the employers in the tool and die business, as well as in the main auto plants, now knew the MESA was a power in its own right, with a membership of over 20,000.

Another union that made an impact on the industrial scene of Detroit in those early days was the Industrial Workers of the World. Joe Brown, who was not a member of the IWW but who held them in high esteem, believed that their struggles in the auto industry were gravely underrated by labor historians. Actually the IWW was active on behalf of auto workers long before the UAW, MESA, and various independent unions sprang up during the thirties. As far back as June 1913 the militancy of the IWW resulted in the Studebaker strike after the company fired a member of a committee elected to discuss grievances. Nearly 6,000 workers in three Detroit Studebaker plants answered the strike call. Their demands: eight hours work for ten hours pay, improved health and safety conditions, no discrimination against strikers after settlement, and payday every week instead of every two weeks. This strike was of historic significance because it was the first strike of an industrial union in the auto industry. The depression year of 1913 was hardly propitious for waging a successful strike. The company agreed to shorten the payday period but conceded to nothing else. At least the strike served to dramatize the problem of organizing workers in a large mass production industry.

Was the IWW responsible for Henry Ford's five-dollar-a-day policy in 1914? Some labor historians think so. Beginning in 1911 the IWW engaged in a recruiting drive in Detroit. In addition to the Studebaker strike, the Wobblies led many minor strikes—always with the same demand: eight hours work for ten hours pay, rehiring of men fired for union activity, and recognition of the shop committee. "The mark of the IWW was an impermanent one but the latest chronicler of the Ford empire believes that the threat of the rising tide of radicalism, in which the Wobblies slammed Ford with large chunks of propaganda, was the cause of his adoption of the five-dollars-a-day policy," wrote George Blackwood in his dissertation.

During the "prosperous" twenties the IWW in Detroit confined its activities mostly to education and agitation. Yet spontaneous strikes of short duration popped up repeatedly during that decade. How "spontaneous" were those strikes? I am reminded that it was the English socialist, Limey, who planted the strike idea in our heads at Continental Motors. How many of the walkouts during the twenties were prompted by radicals, especially IWW members? Who knows? Combing through files in the Wayne State University Labor Archives, I made a random list of "quickie strikes" in the twenties. Here is a partial list of such stoppages, their causes, and results:

June 1926	Hudson Motor—thirty men wanted increase from fifty to fifty-five cents an hour—demand granted but leaders fired.
July 1926	Fisher Body—against wage cut—wages restored but leaders fired.
March 1928	Murray Body—against wage cut—won slight increase; no one fired.
January 1928	Fisher Body Plant 23—tool and die workers—cut in overtime for men working Saturday night—all thirty leaders fired; company refused to adjust dispute.
June 1927	Hudson—dockers of trim shop—for wage increase— all fired.
July 1927	Dodge—water sanders—promise of day work not kept; committee fired.
April 1928	Packard—laid off and rehired at lower rate—all men fired but two suckers who stayed on job and broke in lower-rate men.
January 1927	Budd Wheel—all men in department—60 percent wage cut in this department—men stopped work—all men fired and black list established.

In his *The Automobile Under the Blue Eagle* Sidney Fine wrote:

The IWW made its major effort to win adherents among the automobile workers in the summer and early fall of 1933. In an effort to draw a contrast between itself and the AFL, it directed its appeal to the automobile workers as a militant, rank-and-file controlled industrial union with low dues and initiation fees and open to all workers regardless of their skill, sex, color or nationality. It distributed more than two million pieces of literature during three months, held numerous meetings at plant gates, and even initiated six-days-a-week broadcasts over a Dearborn radio station. In September, Metal and Machinery Workers Industrial Union No. 440 moved its Detroit headquarters into larger quarters: "One Big Union Hall," which the editor of the *Industrial Worker* later described as "A lavish front for the growing union; in the kitchen back of it, the organizers survived on bread and beans and slept on benches."

Joe Brown, who was one of the men who survived on beans and slept on a bench, wrote to me about the Murray Body strike, which was led by the IWW in the fall of 1933:

The IWW leaders tried to counsel the workers that this is not a good time to strike, but the workers voted overwhelmingly for an immediate strike. There are three main demands here: recognition for the union shop committee, a shorter work week, and no discrimination against union members. The Company simply thumbs its nose at the union committee, so every day we picket. Every picket has a Wobbly song book, and we sing all the songs, one after another, even to "Pie in the Sky When You Die." Not far from the picket line is a relief kitchen, so no one goes hungry. The strikers know what scabs still work in the plant. So a "visiting committee" has been set up to call on the scabs in their homes and "persuade" them that it would be healthier to march in the picket line. The scabs usually get the message. Frankly I don't think this strike can be won. The best time to call a strike is in the peak production season, when the company is in a rush to get out orders, not in the slack season when the company reduces its work force.

Shortly after Joe wrote that letter the strike was called off, without netting a single gain.

Sidney Fine quotes F.W. Thompson, the chairman of the strike committee and of the IWW's general executive board: "The loss of the Murray strike was the loss of the campaign in Detroit."

My old friend Harry Riseman, who along with I. Rab introduced me to socialism in 1919 and who later became a successful lawyer, told me recently that he provided legal services for the IWW in 1933: "I urged them to let me negotiate contracts for them with the employers, but they flatly refused. Their motto at that time was: 'No contracts with the bosses, only direct action on the job.' "

When I wrote to Fred Thompson asking for his version of IWW activity in Detroit during 1933, he replied:

Regarding the comments from Sidney Fine that you give in your letter, I would say what I say in my book: the process of organizing or trying to get workers to organize endured through the summer with little results, until at Murray Body, just before changeover of model and consequent reduction of company operations; as workers belatedly began to "hive" around the IWW they found themselves laid off the next week and attributed this to the fact they had joined; this forced the IWW to act; we sought some workable compromise as rotation of work, etc.; and the Murray board refused to go along, though they did meet with us. We pulled the plant. (My lone proposal that day to the committee only, and never getting beyond that, was to pull as we did for a meeting by blowing the whistles and shutting off the power, then proposing giving management one more chance to work something out on the layoffs, either something would have been worked out, or the onus for the continued shutdown would be on the company.) It was a strike we could not win, and it cramped our efforts at various other plants. Through that winter we did our utmost to visit those workers and retain a base, but our "eggs were in one basket" and were smashed.

I have wondered at times how it would have worked out if we had managed to bring the auto industry into the IWW, what change that would have made in the style of the IWW and what changes in the history of American unionism.

FDR Intervenes

The rebellion of the auto workers in 1933 was summed up by Josephine Goman, then on the staff of Mayor Frank Murphy: "The strikes just burst like lightning on the Detroit scene and served as a kind of outlet for all the difficulties the workers were having." The AFL could not afford to stand by and watch such rivals as the Auto Workers Union, the MESA, and the IWW compete to recruit receptive auto workers to their ranks. AFL President William Green sent William Collins, an AFL representative, to Detroit to hasten the organization of auto workers into federal labor unions. Collins' philosophy hardly fitted the mood of auto workers in 1933: "The purpose of organization of the automobile workers in the federal labor unions is to secure for them the maximum economic benefits to which they are entitled under the operation of the National Industrial Recovery Act. In organizing these workers there is no intent to foment, foster or encourage strikes."

Collins went to Detroit at a time when the AFL was denounced by the employers and the daily press. It did not help the prestige of the AFL when the notorious Purple Gang invaded the labor field, notably in the cleaning and dying business. "The labor movement in Detroit regarded it as just another racket, with no ideals and no principles," Collins complained to Green. Collins also discovered it was very difficult to win Negroes over to the federal unions. The blacks were wary of the AFL because they knew only too well how the building unions and other crafts practiced racial discrimination.

But the AFL's major difficulty was internal, not external. The Federation was suffering from near blindness, from craft myopia. Edward Levinson, in his *Rise of the Auto Workers*, summed up the AFL's problem in one paragraph:

These federal locals turned out to be about as worthless as the company unions. They enjoyed no autonomy; they could not bargain, strike, or draw up a contract for themselves. The only secure privilege they had was to pay a per capita tax of 35 cents a month to the AFL. Demands that the auto workers' Federal locals be given the right to federate together into an international, industrial union of their own were denied. The reason was simple: the AFL craft unions had plans of their own—plans to divide up the skilled and semi-skilled workers among the 57 varieties of oldline craft organizations.

Unionization continued, strikes spread, and the auto workers demanded action on a national scale and agitated for a general strike to force union recognition. A.J. Muste, in his *The Automobile Industry and Organized Labor*, claims that over 60,000 were enrolled in federal locals in Detroit and 150,000 elsewhere. The Federation chiefs could no longer ignore the mounting pressure for action and set 20 March 1934 as the date the auto workers were to strike and deal a deathblow to company unionism. However, the AFL leaders yielded to President Franklin Roosevelt's request for a postponement, and on 25 March they accepted a settlement in which Roosevelt personally intervened. Up to that time the auto workers believed that Roosevelt was on their side and that his administration would fully protect their right to organize under Section 7(a) of the NRA and compel the employers to bargain in good faith. But the March 1934 settlement knocked that illusion out of their heads. Muste tells what happened:

For it was Roosevelt in person who wrote into the automobile code the now famous, and to labor and all liberals, the infamous "merit clause" and "proportional representation" provision. The first, by permitting employers equipped with an efficient labor espionage system to discharge men for "incompetency" or "neglect" (that is, to be their own judge of the "merit" of employees), gave these employers the power to fire workers for union activity and to terrorize all the aggressive spirits among them. Then to leave no loop-hole the code provided that on committees for collective bargaining unions, non-AFL company unions should be proportionally represented. Thus the President placed the company union on the same footing as the genuine workers' union and enabled the employers to make sure in advance that the union would not present a united front for bargaining purposes but be

Amid clouds of tear gas, Auto-Lite strikers seek stones to combat the oncoming state troopers. Two were killed and many injured in this melee.

divided into separate jealous and often warring groups. Then the settlement provided for an Automobile Labor Board which would presumably guard against discrimination, guarantee collective bargaining—after the strike had been sabotaged and the effort of the men to forge an instrument, a strong union, to represent them in bargaining had been blocked.

Even the AFL officials had to admit that nothing had been gained and that the Wolman Board was useless. Joe Brown told me that as a result of this disappointing "settlement" thousands of workers in the Detroit federal unions dropped out in disgust. The workers learned the obvious lesson: if they wanted justice they could not depend on the "Little White Father" to hand it down to them on a platter; they had to fight for it. And fight they did!

In the spring of 1934 the Federal Labor Union Number 18384 directed a strike against the Auto-Lite Company in Toledo—a strike which did not end until ten thousand Toledoans had engaged in a four days' pitched battle with deputies, private guards, and militia. In the beginning it seemed as if the strike would be lost. The AFL leaders in the automobile industry gave no help whatever. And the leaders of Local 18384 were too inexperienced to provide able leadership. But help came from the outside—from A.J. Muste's Workers Party and the Lucas County Unemployed League. These organizations reinforced the picket line, set up relief committees, and stiffened the morale of the strikers. The Auto-Lite Company prevailed upon Judge Roy Stuart to issue an injunction against mass picketing. At first the strikers obeyed the injunction, with the result that strikebreakers began to pour into the plant. The Unemployment League promptly notified the judge that they would smash his injunction by peaceful mass picketing.

"From this point forward, the strike, which had appeared lost, was aggressively pursued, and the violence that finally occurred became increasingly predictable," says Sidney Fine in *The Automobile Under the Blue Eagle*. Dramatic events followed as in a fast-moving stage play. On 15 May some 107 persons were arrested for violating the injunction. The following day over 45 persons were arrested, of whom 24 were cited for contempt. Most of those arrested were members of the Unemployment League. With each passing day tension rose. When three additional picketers were arrested on 17 May, a mob of over 200 strikers and sympathizers stormed the jail and threatened to break down the doors and free the three men. The next day Judge Stuart held hearings on the contempt charges while a crowd of strikers and their friends sang in the courthouse corridors. "They sang as lustily as Wobblies jailed in a free speech fight," said Joe Brown, who covered the strike for the Federated Press. Defying court orders, the strikers and their allies blocked the factory entrances, resisted the police, and stopped workers on the day shift from leaving the plant. Rioting broke out when deputies in the plant used gas, guns, and grenades to drive the pickets back. The pickets rushed the plant, smashed windows, tore down fences, and even attempted to set the property on fire. The daily press reported that "a reign of terror" kept 1,800 workers trapped in the plant. A representative of the Cleveland Regional Labor Board reported that not a single window remained in the plant, which prompted a striker to quip: "They want an open shop? Well now they've got one."

Barricades

On 23 May the governor of Ohio ordered the National Guard into Toledo "to save the lives of the beleaguered employees and restore law and order." The strikebreakers who were forced to spend the night in the plant were sent home and the plant was closed, but the pickets remained on guard. When Guardsmen couldn't clear the pickets away with bayonets they threw vomiting gas and tear gas. The strikers ran for cover on the porches of nearby homes and set up barricades. "Fighting between the mob and the troops raged throughout the day of the 24th and then broke out again the following afternoon before an audience that, according to the police estimates, reached twenty thousand in the early evening," writes Fine. The next day violence became more bitter, with guardsmen attacking pickets with bayonets and gas, while the strikers hurled bricks, bottles, and other ammunition. Two strike sympathizers died from militia bullets, dozens of people were injured, many were jailed, and much property near the plant was damaged.

Credit for working out the strategy and tactics of that historic strike must go to the Musteites. As for the Communists, their state organizer, John Williamson, had to admit that "the AWU played no role during the strike due to its prior isolation from the Auto-Lite workers and the trade union movement generally." Ironically, while the employers and their supporters denounced the Musteites as "irresponsible Red agitators," the Communists, with characteristic Third Period logic, vilified the Muste people as "Left Social Fascists." The crafts affiliated with the Toledo Central Labor Council reacted to the use of troops by voting overwhelmingly to call a general strike unless President Roosevelt acted to restore law and order in Toledo. The strike date was set for 2 June. The threat of a general strike alarmed the Roosevelt administration, frightened city officials, and caused poor AFL President Green to wail: "I hardly know what to do in this situation at the present time." Representatives of the National Labor Board, company officials, and union negotiators worked feverishly to effect a settlement before the strike deadline, and they reached one just in time.

On 2 June the National Labor Board was told: "The battle of Toledo is officially settled and the peace treaties in the form of working agreements for a six-month period have been signed." Later A.J. Muste wrote:

The methods employed in the Auto-Lite strike—calm but inexorable defiance of injunctions, cooperation between the unemployed organizations and the unions, dramatization of the strike issue to bring the masses out to observe and participate in picketing, the threat of a local general strike by the city central body, persistent effort by groups of advanced workers with a revolutionary outlook but a realistic union policy—brought the Auto-Lite strike to an end with a partial victory by the union. Before a year passed they led to the complete unionization of the Auto-Lite plant and of the entire auto parts industry in Toledo. In other cities and industries these same methods in many cases applied by workers consciously following the Toledo example brought complete or partial victory on a great series of struggles which made the year 1934 one of the most notable in the history of the American working class.

And in a letter to me Joe Brown wrote prophetically:

After the victory at Auto-Lite nothing can stop the success of unionism in the auto industry. Already there is talk in union circles of striking the Toledo Chevrolet plant. I predict that if and when the strike takes place the workers will win because GM doesn't want a repetition of what happened in Auto-Lite. There will be more strikes in auto centers; some will be lost, some will be partially won, and all of them will be like dress rehearsals for the Big Drama to come—when the workers tackle the General Motors citadel in Flint. During the Auto-Lite strike many of the radicals you and I know in Detroit flocked to Toledo in support of the strikers. These are stirring times, especially for radicals. As you know, leaders don't make events; rather, events make leaders. Every strike brings to prominence new, young militant leaders—guys like George Addes and Bob Travis.

Every time Brown wrote to me in this vein I would pester the doctor when he made his daily rounds. "Doc, when can I get out of this place? Can't something be done to speed up recovery?" His answer was always the same: "When your sputum turns negative we'll set a date for your release. Until then—just take the cure. If you allow yourself to get in a stew you'll only prolong the trouble." But I didn't know how long I would be cooped up in the San. I began to hate everything about the place: the constant smell of iodoform in the infirmary; the pompous manner of some of the head doctors; the hierarchical structure with the doctors at the top, the interns on the next rung below, then the nurses, the nurses' aides, and finally the orderlies at the bottom. "It's like in a damn army," a nurse told me once, "you take orders from those above you and give orders to those below you." When someone hemorrhaged or died, the news spread through the San in a flash. A patient remarked, "Did you hear? So and so was carried out in a basket last night. I knew the poor guy couldn't last much longer; he was just wasting away, must have had galloping consumption." Then the patients who heard the news launched into a morbid discussion about death. Most of the patients were working-class people and possessed typical working-class attitudes. I missed the opportunity for stimulating discussion of the kind we used to engage in when I belonged to the Marxian Club in Detroit. I found my outlet in reading, but one can't read all the time. There were days when I felt insufferably bored and depressed. I ached for the time when I could return to Detroit and become active in the union movement.

First Convention

When the top-ranking AFL officials realized they could no longer contain the growing demand for a national union of auto workers, William Green announced that a convention would be held in Detroit in August 1935. How I wished I could have attended that convention! When Brown sent me a copy of the convention proceedings I read them over and over. I was dumfounded to learn that AFL President Green appointed all the officers and executive board members. I wrote to Brown: "In reading the proceedings, I gather that Green succeeded in thwarting the delegates on the two basic issues: jurisdiction and autonomy. The delegates wanted the UAW to have jurisdiction over all workers engaged in auto production, regardless of skill. And they wanted the right to elect their own international officers. But Green imposed the will of the AFL executive council on the convention, with the result that: (1) the new union in effect had jurisdiction over production workers but not over the skilled workers, and (2) Green used his full powers to appoint the top officers and executive board members. One does not have to be a prophet to predict that at the next convention both of these decisions will be reversed."

Brown also kept me informed about three significant Detroit developments in 1935: the Motor Products strike and the formation of two independent unions—the Automobile Industrial Workers Association (AIWA) and the Associated Automotive Workers of America (AAWA). The AIWA was first organized in the Dodge plant and later recruited members in other plants. The AAWA centered mainly in the Hudson plant. I was always intensely interested to learn about organizing developments in plants where I had worked, such as Motor Products, Dodge, and Hudson. The Motor Products strike showed what confusion and disruption can occur when several unions become involved in a strike. The UAW, the AIWA, the MESA, and the Metal Polishers Union all had members in the plant. Company officials used the excuse that they could not bargain because they did not know which union spoke for the employees. Francis Dillon, an AFL hack whom Green appointed president of the UAW, declared that the strike had no possible chance of success and ordered the UAW members back to work. The MESA and AIWA continued the strike, but eventually they had to admit defeat. The MESA's official organ blasted Dillon as a Judas and strikebreaker. Clearly the situation in Detroit called for a merger of the independents and the UAW. The merger came when the UAW held its second convention in April 1936; the AIWA and the AAWA became part of the UAW, but the MESA remained independent. Incidentally, I was always amused when international UAW representatives at summer school sessions insisted that the UAW dates from the 1936 convention, presumably because Walter Reuther was a delegate to that convention, though he had not been on the auto scene in 1935.

Goodby to Iola

Two years passed and in 1935 I was still incarcerated in the San. In the summer of 1934 I sensed a change in Mary. I could see that her patience was wearing thin. Late in that year she consulted Dr. Bridge about my case. All he could say was that my x-ray showed improvement, "but no one except God can give you a definite date for his recovery." Since Mary didn't believe in God she did not bother to ask Him, but she clearly decided it was hopeless to continue our relationship, and I certainly couldn't blame her. In February 1935 she left Rochester to take a job in New York City. For some time she was active in the New York branch of the Workers' Socialist Party, now the World Socialist Party. Later she joined the Council Communists, for which Paul

Mattick, a profound Marxist, was the moving spirit. During World War II, I was dumfounded to learn she had joined the Army to become a WAC. A few years after the war ended she enrolled in Indiana University, but I do not know how long she continued her studies there. I was told she repudiated socialism completely.

My last year in the San was 1935. Two memorable events happened to me in that year: my sputum turned negative, indicating the disease had been arrested at last, and thanks to Arthur Rosenberg's *History of Bolshevism* I lost my illusions about the nature of the Soviet system. Rosenberg convinced me that Russia is in no sense a "workers' state" and not even a "degenerated workers' state," but an exploitative society ruled by a bureaucratic elite, and Russia therefore had nothing in common with democratic socialism. I resolved that when I got back into circulation, I would join the party of Norman Thomas.

Early in 1936 I bid Iola Sanatorium goodby and began the painful experience of readjusting to the outside world. I moved to Detroit and temporarily lived with my sister's family. Like thousands of other small business owners, her husband suffered economic reverses and the family was in straitened circumstances. I was determined to find employment as quickly as possible. I joined the Socialist Party, which in those days had two lively branches in Detroit. When I learned that Melvin Bishop, a party member, served as the education director of the fledgling United Auto Workers union and that his wife, Dorothy, was director of the Works Progress Administration Workers' Education Program, I lost no time applying for a job on the federal project. Dorothy told me she could hire me but I first had to get on the public welfare rolls. After replying to all the humiliating questions and filling out all the forms, I had to wait six weeks before the welfare department put through the okay.

It was a happy day for me when Dorothy officially added me to her staff. Old-timers will recall how cartoonists and comedians then poked fun at WPA "boondogglers." To me, however, workers' education was not boondoggling, but a labor of love which was to last more than thirty years.

5 On WPA

Since the mid-sixties there has been a spate of books by writers who spelled out their disenchantment with the trade union movement. There was nothing disenchanting about the UAW in those early days; to the contrary, the sit-down strikes, wildcat strikes, factional fights, turbulent conventions, and rambunctious membership meetings during the decade 1937 to 1947 formed a chapter in labor history the like of which will never be seen again.

My very first assignment in workers' education was filled with excitement. I spoke at a membership meeting of the Graham-Paige Local on the subject of workers' education and outlined the topics of a six-session course on the "Principles of Unionism." I called for a show of hands to see how many members would attend such a course in the local. At least fifty hands went up. Then the local's recording secretary, who had been diligently taking notes while I spoke, asked for the floor and proceeded to discredit everything I had said. He reeled off reasons as to why members of the local did not "need any professors to tell them how to run our union; we did pretty well so far, and professors would only muddle our people." His diatribe touched off a bitter exchange between the few members who agreed with him and the majority who booed them.

The meeting was becoming increasingly turbulent and the president banged his gavel on the table and shouted for order. Then something happened that stunned the workers in that hall. Dick Frankensteen, then a UAW executive board member, and his aide, Morris Field, walked into the hall, went up on the platform, and whispered something to the local's president. The president turned pale, walked to the edge of the platform and said, "Brothers and sisters, Brother Frankensteen has something to tell us." The workers listened with amazement as Frankensteen explained how the La Follette Civil Liberties Committee discovered that the local's recording secretary was being paid by an espionage agency to send in written reports about the union's affairs and the activities of key union members. After making his report, Frankensteen urged the workers to refrain from harming the recording secretary: "His conscience will punish him enough." The next day, the recording secretary quit his factory job and left town. Similar spy disclosures occurred in other UAW locals in those days.

One of my duties was to promote classes in local unions, and this gave me an opportunity to observe auto workers in action. Reams have been written about the militant spirit of auto workers during the CIO upsurge. Sidney Fine's well-documented story of the General Motors sit-down strike of 1936–37 gives a graphic account of that militancy and solidarity. Several times during December and January of that winter I went to Flint to deliver talks on "What Means This Strike." (That title was coined by Daniel De Leon for one of his pamphlets. In those days, I used quotes from socialist classics the way a preacher uses quotes from the Bible.)

I always arranged to ride with a group of Chrysler workers, who, after working eight hours on the night shift, piled into cars and drove from Detroit to Flint to lend support to the strike in whatever way they could—helping out in the kitchen, passing out leaflets, marching before the plants to show their solidarity with the sit-downers, ready at the drop of a hat to battle police or even National Guardsmen if the sit-downers were attacked. Workers from Pontiac, Toledo, and other auto centers formed similar caravans and sang—"On To Flint!" I also gave talks to sit-down strikers in the Plymouth and Dodge truck plants during the 1937 Chrysler strike. One time I took young Gus Tyler to the Plymouth plant, where I introduced him as "a labor writer and lecturer." Gus, then a left-of-center member of the Socialist Party and editor of the *Call*, made one of the best twenty-minute inspirational talks that I ever heard.

Midland Steel

What a difference there is between the way strikes were conducted in those days and the way they are conducted now! A case in point was the Midland Steel strike in Detroit. One of the chief leaders of the strike was John Anderson, an able Scotsman with a rich brogue who in the 1930s ran for governor on the Communist Party ticket and who later helped to organize skilled workers in Detroit tool and die shops. During the factional fight, he was a sharp thorn in the side of the Reuther forces, but when the postwar anti-communist drive got under way John lost his union post. His remarkable negotiating ability led a tool and die employers' association to hire him as their labor relations expert. A UAW International representative told me: "Although John is now on the other side of the bargaining table, he is fair; he will not let the company cheat us in terms of the contract, and he won't let us pull anything over on the company." Someone said that "for the first twenty-five years of his adult life, John was a hell-raiser; today he is a respected citizen and church-goer in an affluent community." I recall so well how John functioned in the Midland Steel strike.

John was a member of the Midland bargaining committee. Always after the committee met with the company, John called a membership meeting and reported in detail what took place. Then he called for instructions from the workers. Repeatedly I heard him say: "Remember, YOU are the union; YOU call the shots; YOU decide what is to be done!" Every afternoon a membership meeting was called to discuss the latest strike developments. When contract terms were hammered out by management and the union bargaining committee, the local officers called a special ratification meeting of the entire membership. The chairman of the bargaining committee read each sentence of the tentative agreement and then asked for questions and critical comments. If the workers voted to accept the company's terms, the strike ended; if they rejected the terms, the strike continued, and the two parties returned to the bargaining table.

How often recently have I heard local presidents and international union representatives parrot the cliché: "The UAW is a union of, for, and by the membership!" When the UAW was young that statement was not a cliché but a fact. At Midland I observed how workers—who in pre-union days were mute, faceless automatons in the plants—were learning from their daily strike experiences. They were learning how to serve on committees, how to make reports, write leaflets, interpret contract clauses, and, above all else, how to talk back to arrogant and demanding supervisors. Once at a discussion meeting I asked a young woman striker why she joined the union. I thought she would cite better wages as her main reason. I was wrong. She said: "When you belong to a union, the foreman can't screw you. Last month my foreman asked me to go out with him. I told him 'to hell with you, Charlie, I know what you want.' He got mad, but he didn't try to spite me. He knew damn well the union would be on his neck if he did."

Dorothy Hubbard assigned me to be one of the instructors at the 1937 summer school at Woodland Lake, Michigan. What a primitive setting! What rudimentary instructions! Someone should write a story titled "The UAW—From Woodland Lake to Black Lake." A UAW brochure has this to say about Black Lake: "Walter Reuther was determined to make the UAW Family Education Center an education retreat to compare favorably with any in the country. You cannot imagine how well he succeeded until you see the center. Its architecture is stunning. Inside, the decor and appointments are the finest quality. Outside, you will see landscape painstakingly done to preserve nature's bounty to the maximum." Today at Black Lake expert instructors and discussion leaders are using the latest sophisticated techniques to conduct sessions in topics like collective bargaining, time study, economics, psychology, and political campaigning.

How different was the 1937 summer school, housed in an old abandoned hunting lodge. There was no wall-to-wall carpeting, no Danish furniture, no large indoor swimming pool, no sleeping and eating facilities that compare favorably with the best modern motels. Instead, our old hunting lodge had crude makeshift sleeping quarters on the second floor, where the students slept on cots instead of innerspring mattress beds. The big room downstairs had to serve as classroom, dining room, and recreation hall. The women slept on the west side of the second floor, the men on the east side, and in the wee hours of the morning there would be Romeo and Juliet flirtations across the balconies that separated the two sections. With such antics going on, one got little sleep, so after a few days I bought a tent and pitched it under an apple tree some distance from the lodge.

Nor was there anything sophisticated about the instructions imparted at that early summer school. We were not trained discussion leaders like those at Black Lake today. We tried so hard to elicit discussion from the students. "I can't get them to talk in my labor history class, they're so green," complained Joel Seidman, a former instructor at Brookwood Labor College. Boaz Siegal (now a labor lawyer) found a way to make his charges talk in his parliamentary law class. He set up a mock union meeting and wrote out what each student had to say—one made a motion, another seconded it, another spoke in favor, another in opposition, and so on.

I was lucky, for I was picked to conduct the class in grievance procedure. Shop problems—no trouble getting them to talk about that!

None of the other instructors had ever worked in an auto shop. I thought up problems based on my past factory experiences and told the students to write them up as grievances. Then I divided the group into two sides; one side to act as the union and the other side to act as management. The opposing teams went at each other hammer and tongs. Since those days the methods of workers' education have been improved and refined—but the underlying principle is the same as it was in that 1937 grievance procedure course. Any subject, whether collective bargaining or psychology or labor history or whatever, can be made meaningful to workers if it is presented in a way that makes sense in terms of their experience. Workers don't think in abstractions, but in terms of the concrete.

We had something at Woodland Lake that you won't find at Black Lake today. I refer to the spirit, the elan, the fervor, the warm feeling of fraternity that was so evident in the way they sang. Every night they sang the whole repertory of union songs. They sang with feeling—the kind of feeling black people conveyed when they marched behind Martin Luther King singing "We Shall Overcome."

6 Dodge Local 3

The WPA Workers' Education Program folded in the fall of 1937. The daily press carried front-page stories about how the government program was riddled with Communists who were teaching Red doctrines to unsuspecting union members. The *Detroit Free Press* carried a picture of a class I conducted in a Plymouth local. On the same page was a feature story about Communist infiltration in the WPA. The story was grossly exaggerated, for actually, there was only one Communist Party member on our program. In September of that year, I taught my last class under WPA auspices. One month later I was hired as full-time education director of UAW Dodge Local 3, which at that time had 30,000 members.

I began my duties in Dodge Local 3 about six months after Chrysler workers won union recognition. During the four years I worked for that local I was able to observe at first hand how auto workers ran their union in those early days. The Dodge local offered a good case study. In 1968 I interviewed a number of old-time Dodge workers who participated in the very first organizing attempts in 1933–34 and continued their union activities until they retired. From those interviews I pieced together the story, and I am setting it down here as it was told to me. A composite Dodge worker speaks as follows:

To give you an idea of what it was like to work in the Dodge plant before we had a union, let me begin with the 1934 model changeover. In those days, there was no such thing as seniority, and foremen were not required to rehire workers on call-back. But there was a sure way for a laid-off worker to get rehired when production started on the new model. All he had to do was to slip the foreman some dough—and this is exactly what many workers did, especially married men with families to support. When we went back to work in 1934 we found that the pay rates had been cut, and when we complained we were told, "If you don't want to work, just remember that any one of those guys in that long line of job hunters at the employment office will be only too glad to take your place." It was around that time that the Automobile Labor Board was set up under the National Industrial Recovery Act to mediate labor-management disputes in the auto industry.

This board created a so-called representation system in auto plants, including our Dodge plant. Half of the members represented the workers and half represented management. What a joke! We could win petty grievances like getting a broken window pane replaced, but on major grievances, such as pay rates or speedup or health hazards, all we got was the runaround. So we got fed up with that company union arrangement and decided to form an independent union. And that's how the Automotive Industrial Workers Association (AIWA) was born. At first it was centered in the Dodge plant, but it soon spread to other Chrysler plants and to some independent parts plants. It was called a two-bit union because dues were twenty-five cents per month; however, we soon realized we needed more resources, and dues were raised to fifty cents. We were in competition with the AFL, which was trying to build its federal locals of auto workers. In August 1935 the AFL called a conference of auto workers in Detroit and granted a charter forming the United Automobile Workers of America. However, AFL President William Green appointed all the officers.

Auto workers took a dim view of a union that had no autonomy, and the membership of the UAW declined. The AFL soon realized it could not keep the UAW bottled and corked forever and announced that an election of officers was to take place at a convention in South Bend, Indiana, in April 1936. Our AIWA sent a representative to that convention to explore the possibility of joining the UAW. What an encouraging report he brought back! At a packed AIWA membership meeting, he told how the AFL was literally forced to bow out and how the convention delegates elected their own officers and formed their own policies. Three months later we dissolved our AIWA and went into the UAW. We lost no time letting the company know we wanted union recognition and the right to process grievances. Management replied by becoming more arrogant. In the fall model changeover, nearly 500 workers were notified that they would not be rehired. The UAW put on the pressure and called on the CIO for help. Philip Murray of the CIO came to Detroit to meet with Chrysler management, but to no avail. He warned the corporation that the CIO would launch a nationwide boycott of Chrysler products unless the men were called back to work. At first company officials laughed at the threat, but later they decided it was no joke and called all the workers back on their jobs. But our top priority was the demand for union recognition, for exclusive bargaining rights. Repeatedly we met with management and each time they stalled. Fed up with such stalling tactics, the UAW called a strike and closed seven Chrysler plants on 8 March 1937.

This brief account by a "composite worker" points up the progress made by Dodge employees from the company union representation

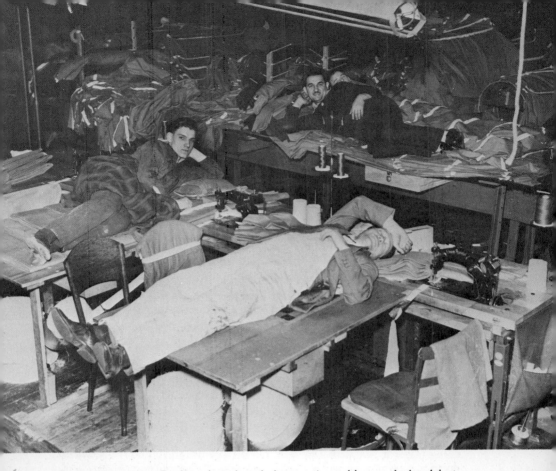

These men of the Dodge plant found that sewing tables made hard but satisfactory beds.

plan to the sit-down strike which forced Chrysler to grant union recognition and to sign a contract on 6 April 1937. I was still on the WPA staff when the strike occurred and was assigned to conduct a class in "strike strategy and tactics" in the Dodge local, so I know how the sit-down strikers operated. Invariably when workers take over a plant or a city (during a general strike), they set up committees. This was the first thing the sit-downers did in the Dodge plant. A plant protection committee was delegated to see that no damage was done to company property. A member of that committee told me, "By protecting the machines, we were protecting our jobs." The policing committee was responsible for maintaining discipline; anyone caught with booze was ejected from the plant, as were "stool pigeons, rabble rousers, and other trouble makers." (Several stool pigeons were caught in the act of phoning reports to the company.) Clean-up squads and scrub gangs gave the plant a new look. As one striker put it: "We had to clean the windows so we could see outside; they were so thick with grime that workers could not tell whether they were working the day or the night shift." Food was brought to the plant by a caterer and a food committee supervised the mealtime arrangements.

An investigating committee lost no time checking company records for espionage data. They found plenty. From 1935 to 1937 the company systematically recorded the activities of every key unionist, citing what time he went to the toilet, how long he stayed, what he said, how many times he was absent or came to work late, whether he passed out union literature and if so what kind, and so on. Other committees handled recreation, education, entertainment, and publicity. The Dodge sit-down strike, like other sit-down strikes in those days, became a model of workers' control—not control of production, but control of the plant. Here is how a Dodge worker, whose history I recorded on tape, explained what workers did after the settlement:

Once we got our first contract, we set about improving the working conditions. First we had to cut down to size those hard-boiled foremen, who over the years formed the habit of acting like autocrats whose word was law. Now they had to deal with our stewards, and this was hard for them to take, especially when we challenged them on production standards. We told them the contract called for a fair day's work for a fair day's pay, and by God a fair day's work was all they were going to get. We often had a hard time getting our own people to slow down; they had been so used to working at a fast speed that they couldn't adjust to a slower pace. So we told them to take a walk from time to time and not turn out more work than the rest of us did. And we damn soon put a stop to the way some Polish foremen used to curse in Polish to intimidate and speed up Poles on the production line. We also put a stop to foremen turning out production. They used to roll up their sleeves and work like hell on the line or on a machine. We told them that if they wanted extra work turned out, they should hire extra workers. At first they ignored us. So every time they turned out work, we simply turned out less work. Sometimes foremen would jerk up the automatic conveyor a couple notches and speed up the line. We cured them of that practice; we simply let jobs go by half-finished. Make no mistake about it; in those days our stewards had power.

Factional Fights

Today local union officers complain that all too often not enough workers attend union meetings to make up a quorum. When I worked in the Dodge local, every membership meeting was jam-packed—and nearly always stormy. After the 1937 UAW convention, the factional fight raged in every local union, notably in large locals like Dodge Local 3. On the one side was the "unity" group, whose leading strategists included members of the SP, CP, ACTU (Associated Catholic Trade Unionists), and able union militants like George Addes. I wonder how many UAW historians know that the Trotskyites were in the Homer Martin camp in 1938. I know how it happened: in the spring of 1938 Morris Field, then a UAW executive board member and international education director, asked me to accompany him to New York to meet union education experts. Among the people we interviewed were Mark Starr, education director of the International Ladies Garment Workers Union, and Lewis Corey and Will Herberg, who were also on the education staff of the ILGWU. From those men I got some valuable ideas that helped me improve my own education methods later.

But I soon learned that Field, who was then a Homer Martin supporter (he switched to the other side later), had another reason for making the trip to New York—a factional reason. He reported to Jay Lovestone about the factional situation in Detroit and suggested how the Lovestoneites could become more effective in the Martin camp. That was the only time I ever saw Lovestone, and I can still remember how his face twisted in hate every time he hissed: "The filthy Stalinist lice are crawling all over the UAW; they must be stamped out!" After his meeting with Lovestone, Field contacted Jim Cannon, leader of the Trotskyites, and worked out a deal with him. Cannon insisted that the Stalinists in the UAW had to be defeated at all costs and agreed that his group would help Martin. Cannon proposed that Bert Cochran, an able member of his group, be put on Martin's payroll; Field assured him that that could be arranged, and it was.

During 1937–38, the Detroit Socialist Party had two branches; those of us who were active in the UAW belonged to Branch 2; non-UAW members—lawyers, teachers, small businessmen, and others—belonged to Branch 1. The two branches did not take kindly to each other. Members of Branch 1 stood four-square in favor of adhering strictly to Socialist Party policy regarding political action and believed the SP should run its own candidates in local, state, and national elections. Members of Branch 2, however, were in a dilemma. In 1938, the UAW strongly supported Governor Frank Murphy, who was running for re-election on the Democratic ticket. Most Branch 2 members insisted that we support Murphy. "How can we do effective work in the union if we openly oppose candidates officially endorsed by the union?," they asked. I was among the minority (considered by the majority to be a hopeless "sectarian") who argued that Socialists must at all times support SP candidates and expose the Democratic Party and its politicians, including Murphy.

I know from painful experience how we "sectarians" found ourselves in an untenable position. When word got around in the Dodge local that "Marquart is against Governor Murphy," the local's executive board asked me to speak at the next membership meeting and "let our members know where you stand with respect to Governor Murphy." To prepare for that talk, I spent many hours gathering information about the policies pursued by Murphy when he was mayor of Detroit during the depth of the depression and, later, when he was governor of Michigan at the time of the General Motors sit-down strike. On the basis of his record, I could show that Murphy, as mayor of Detroit, did as much to relieve distress of the unemployed as any mayor could possibly have done in a large city that was practically broke. Then I explained how Murphy, when the weight of institutionalized industry was brought down on his back, held his ground and refused to order the National Guard to clear the strikers out of GM plants in a bloodbath. I concluded by saying: "Workers must judge Governor Murphy—as they must judge all candidates running for office—on the basis of his record."

I was roundly applauded. Then a Trotskyite jumped up and asked for a point of special privilege to comment on my remarks. He proceeded to pooh-pooh the idea that Murphy refused to use the National Guard and smash the strike. He argued heatedly that "Murphy refused to unleash the National Guard, not because he was on the side of the workers, but because GM did not want him to. Not only would the strikers have destroyed millions of dollars worth of equipment, but workers from all over Michigan and Ohio poured into Flint, prepared to die in defense of the sit-downers. The company knew there would have been such a slaughter that GM would be hated by working people all over the world for a long time to come. So, don't give credit for that union victory to a Democratic politician like Murphy."

His remarks brought boos and catcalls and denunciation. (I never ceased to be amazed at the way Trotskyites had the guts to take unpopular stands at every union meeting, knowing full well their comments would arouse the wrath of the membership.) Was there more truth to what the Trotskyite said than admirers of Murphy would care to admit? In reviewing Sidney Fine's *Sit-Down—The General Motors Strike of 1936–37,* some writers claim he gave Murphy far more credit than he deserved for his part in the victory over GM. I think so, too, for I know how those strikers and their fellow workers from other auto centers felt. They were convinced that if GM and the forces of law could crush the strike, then the union would be defeated in every auto town in the country. If the militia had been used against the sit-downers, the strike would have erupted into an insurrection. General Motors did not want that to happen. Neither did Governor Murphy. And neither did John L. Lewis.

The SP

Sometimes Branches 1 and 2 of the Detroit Socialist Party met jointly to consider an important policy laid down by the national executive committee. Always at those joint sessions there was heated controversy between members of the two branches. Manuel Seidler, a lawyer (and father of Murray Seidler, author of a scholarly biography of Norman Thomas) accused members of Branch 2 of undermining the Socialist Party to promote their activities in the UAW. And able spokesmen of Branch 2, like Leonard Woodcock and Billie Lamson, accused Seidler and his supporters of being too far removed from workers to form intelligent judgments about the role Socialists should play in the union. Some of the comrades almost came to blows when members of Branch 1 accused Walter Reuther of becoming "too footsy" with the CP faction in the UAW. At another time, nasty bickering between members of the two branches was touched off over the issue of beer! The Detroit SP was planning a big social evening to which the public was to be invited, especially UAW people. A teacher in Branch 1 insisted that only nonalcoholic beverages be served. Billie Lamson jumped up: "How in hell do you expect to attract auto workers if you don't have beer!" To which the teacher replied: "If they can't drink soda pop, let them stay away." The argument between the pro-beer and the anti-beer forces ended in the two sides yelling at each other. I can't recall which side won.

Branch 2 counted among its members some of the able young men destined to play important roles in the UAW: the three Reuther brothers—Walter, Roy, and Victor—and Leonard Woodcock, Emil Mazey, Bob Kanter, George Edwards, Billie Lamson, Ben Fischer, Stoyan Menton, Kermit and Genora Johnson, and others. I learned to my dismay that being well-read in the socialist classics does not necessarily prepare one for union leadership. I envied the way these people, all still in their twenties, could analyze the latest union developments, anticipate the next moves of the Martin-Lovestone forces, formulate strategy, and catch their opponents off guard at union membership meetings by introducing proposals that were readily adopted by the workers. And they were always a bane to the Stalinists, for they could expose the Party line smuggled into resolutions proposed by CP members at union meetings. They were also cordially hated by the Lovestoneites. Once Bill Munger, who was Martin's research director and a leading Lovestoneite, told me: "You social democrats are an insidious influence in this union—you are playing right into the hands of the Stalinists!" To a Lovestoneite, the term "social democrat" was a dirty word. But those young Turks in Branch 2 were equally disliked by their comrades in Branch 1. Manny Seidler shouted at me during a discussion we had in a restaurant: "Walter Reuther is a power-hungry bastard who wants to become president of the UAW, and those guys around him like Woodcock and Mazey are opportunists who are using the Socialist Party as a training ground to promote their union careers!" How prophetic he was!

Reuther Slugged

Walter Reuther still attended SP meetings in 1938, though not regularly, since he was becoming increasingly involved in his duties as president of UAW Local 174. In the spring of that year a number of SP members were invited to meet in Walter and May Reuther's apartment to discuss the activities of the CP and the Lovestoneites in the UAW. Attending the meeting were Walter and his wife, May; Victor Reuther and his wife, Sophie; George Edwards (now a federal appeals court judge); Al King, a production worker in a gear plant; Tucker Smith (later Norman Thomas's running mate in the 1948 presidential campaign); Ben Fischer (then a Detroit SP organizer) and his wife, Hanna; Louis Steigerwald, a Fisher Body tool and die maker; Roy Reuther; Robert Kanter; and myself. Since the incident happened over thirty years ago, I have only a dim recollection of what we talked about, but one thing stands out in my mind: George Edwards was holding up a Lovestone paper and ridiculing the dull make-up, its small headlines, long-winded articles, long unbroken columns, and so on. I also recall that May phoned a restaurant and ordered chop suey brought to the apartment.

After that order had been placed, someone knocked on the door, and we naturally thought the chop suey had arrived. But when Walter opened the door, two plug-uglies walked in with drawn guns and ordered us to hold up our hands. One of the goons kept us covered with his revolver. Most of us were standing in the living room, but King, Sophie, and Steigerwald were in the kitchen, near the living room and in plain view of one gunman. The other goon walked over to Walter, put his gun in his pocket, took out a blackjack, and proceeded to beat Walter over the head. A tussle followed; somehow Walter was either knocked down or slid down on the floor in a sitting position, trying to ward off the blows. Suddenly, he grabbed the blackjack with his left hand. The goon tried to jerk it out of Walter's hand and in the struggle the strap broke. Walter now had the business end of the blackjack and quickly tossed it across the room. The goon picked up a lamp from a small table and hit Walter over the head with it; the lamp shattered.

While all this was taking place, the rest of us were standing with our hands up. The goon who covered us kept clicking his gun threateningly. Once he ordered Tucker Smith to move back. Smith was only a few feet in front of the goon, who probably feared that Smith might lunge at him. Sophie picked up a vinegar bottle from the kitchen table and threw it at the goon. When the bottle landed on the floor, I felt as if I had been hit in the stomach. I was sure the goon would start shooting, but he didn't. His face hardened and he warned that if anything like that happened again, someone would get shot.

I don't know how Al King managed to edge over to the kitchen window and jump out, but he did (the apartment was on the second floor). He ran down the street calling for help. The goon who covered us nodded to his pal, indicating they had better leave. As the other goon walked toward the door, he picked up a small stool and threatened to hit Victor over the head with it. Ben Fischer warned, "We are not going to stand by and let some of our friends get killed. Some of us will get shot, but you guys will get hurt, too." As soon as the goons left the apartment George phoned the police, and soon two plainclothesmen came to get the story. Several days later the goons were apprehended. They were tried before a jury on a charge of entry with intent to kill. The defense contended that Walter had paid the two men "to put on an act so he could get publicity." Walter's union factional opponents also circulated this story, but anyone who was in Reuther's apartment when the goons came knows that the charge was preposterous. Nevertheless, the defendants were acquitted. The Ford Motor Company, particularly Harry Bennett's notorious service department, was thought to be behind the affair. And the brilliant young lawyer who handled the defense was believed to be in some way associated with the Ford Company.

Clash of Ideas

May Reuther had been a schoolteacher until she quit her job to become Walter's secretary in Local 174. She was very interested in workers' education and at one time, when she and I discussed this subject at length, she said: "Workers' education should be conducted on three operational levels: (1) tool courses like grievance procedure, public speaking, parliamentary law, and so on; (2) visual aids like pertinent movies shown at membership meetings; and (3) lectures and forums to encourage the exchange of controversial ideas." I told her what Lewis Corey said when I interviewed him in New York: "Top union officials are afraid of controversial ideas—that's why they are afraid of any kind of workers' education that goes beyond vocational training (tool courses) and indoctrination of official policies." May laughed: "That may be true of those bureaucratic AFL unions but certainly does not apply to the UAW!" What she said was true during the early years of the UAW. But later, alas, it became a different story.

It's been a long time since any UAW local staged the no-holds-barred, give-and-take type of discussions we featured in Local 3, like the debate between Tucker Smith and Nat Ganley, two formidable debaters. Nat Ganley was said to be the best CP floor leader in the UAW, and he was highly skilled and persuasive as an advocate of the Party line. At that time, the CP advocated a united front of communists, socialists, liberals (including liberal small businessmen)—"a united front against fascism." Tucker calmly told the audience what such a united front would mean. He named all the Democratic Party mayors who were on the side of employers during strikes. A statistical economist by profession, Tucker was able to present an imposing array of facts and figures to show that Ganley's "liberal small capitalists" were among the worst labor exploiters in the country. Nat Ganley was furious. He resorted to all the unprincipled debating tricks for which Stalinists are noted: sarcasm, sneers, name calling, innuendoes, and downright lies.

When the debate ended, I, as chairman, called for questions and comments from the audience. Hands went up all over the large hall. I have sponsored many debates and participated in many, and I am convinced that debates seldom change opinions but just sharpen issues. Those who agreed with Ganley asked questions and directed their remarks to embarrass Smith. And those who agreed with Smith tried to put Ganley on the spot.

I promoted quite a number of such debates in Local 3 and later conducted follow-up discussions. We discussed, pro and con, the main points made by the debaters and tried to evaluate them in terms of whether they could stand the test of facts and logic. I felt those sessions were always more rewarding than the debates.

Also more profitable than debates were the lectures I scheduled in Local 3. Scott Nearing drew a large crowd when he spoke on the raging Spanish Civil War. Since the majority of Local 3 members were Catholics, I warned Nearing beforehand that he might stir up a hornets' nest. But my fears were unfounded; Nearing did a masterly job of analyzing the social forces in Spain and showing why workers know instinctively that fascism is their deadly enemy.

Another speaker who made a big hit was Norman Thomas when he spoke at the local tool and die unit meeting one Sunday morning. When he began by saying he would talk about the depression, I anticipated a dry talk on economics; instead, his talk sparkled with humorous anecdotes, colorful illustrations, and striking examples to show how big business corporations were practicing "industrial birth control."

The local's officers raised their eyebrows when they learned that I invited Bill Gebert, the CP's Michigan labor representative, to speak. Gebert's talk pleased everyone in the audience except me. He glorified FDR and castigated the "economic royalists who are joining the reactionaries in Congress to undermine the New Deal." In accordance with the CP line, he gave a conspiratorial explanation for the economic nosedive that began in the fall of 1937 and lasted through 1938. He said it was a Wall Street plot.

Another able speaker was a representative of the ACTU who talked about the Industry Council Plan which at that time was being promoted by Catholics, including the CIO's Philip Murray. The plan called for a tripartite setup of labor, management, and government. Jim Waldon, a brilliant maverick who had been at one time or another in the CP as well as in different Trotsky sects and even in the World Socialist Party, and who was too much of an individualistic anarchist to fit into any group, made things lively by comparing the Industry Council Plan with the Italian fascist syndicalist structure. The speaker and the ACTU members in the audience denounced Jim, but he held his ground, with eager assistance from Communists and Trotskyites in the audience.

Every forum meeting we had in those days was well attended, every topic under discussion was controversial, and nearly everyone participated either by asking questions or by making five-minute speeches. How often have I heard Walter Reuther, when speaking on public platforms or over the air, call for "the free exchange of opinions in the market place of ideas!" The time when UAW locals could sponsor free exchange of ideas has long passed—and I'll explain why later.

Visual Aids

I also learned to use movies as an effective educational medium. In 1938 Bill Davenport was UAW assistant education director under Morris Field, his brother-in-law. Davenport became active in the labor movement in Scotland and was still a young man when he emigrated to Canada, where he joined the Marxist Socialist Party. This Party consisted largely of self-educated workers, some of whom contributed theoretical articles to the *Western Clarion*, a lively socialist paper. When Davenport came to Detroit in 1914 he and a number of English socialists formed a Marxian Party in the Motor City. When the writer Jack London resigned from the Socialist Party because of "its lack of emphasis on the class struggle," Davenport wrote a letter congratulating London for parting company with the "reformist SP" and explaining how he and his comrades were striving to "build a party founded on sound revolutionary principles." London wrote an encouraging reply and said that Davenport and his followers were on the right road.

His "Party" never became more than a small sect and Davenport, a down-to-earth practical guy, turned his attention in other directions. I first heard about him during the depression when he took a leading part in a Detroit Unemployment Council and was severely beaten by goons (those were the days when members of the Michigan Black Legion terrorized union organizers and others whom they considered dangerous Reds). Although not a Lovestoneite himself, Davenport engaged in union activities directed by Lovestoneites in New York City. When he started to work in the UAW education department, he prevailed upon Field to set up a kind of "labor college"—a school to teach workers how to teach other workers.

The training staff consisted of Field, Davenport, and John Eldon, a former miner who received a scholarship from his union for a two-year course at Ruskin Labor College. When England suffered from large unemployment during the twenties, Eldon came to Detroit and found work in an auto plant. I first met him when he joined the Proletarian Party and conducted a class in "A Worker Looks at History." He was a competent instructor and his class was always well attended. Little wonder that when Field became UAW education director he promptly added Eldon to his staff. That early teacher-training college was an interesting experiment, and during the time it lasted (it died when the split occurred between the Martin group and the Reuther-Addes-Frankensteen group), a number of rank and file workers received enough basic training to become union leaders. I often called on Eldon and Davenport to speak at the Dodge local membership meetings and their short talks were well received.

But the man who helped me most was Davenport; he had the imagination to see endless possibilities for workers' education in visual aids, especially films. "Nothing makes an impact like films—neither graphs, nor charts, nor slides," he said. One day I suggested that he and I use Dodge Local 3 as a "laboratory" to experiment with films.

Our first project was an outdoor film program in a small park near the Dodge local hall. We used a superb film on housing which we borrowed from WPA and which depicted the acute shortage of low-cost housing in contrast to the available middle-class housing. We hooked up a loudspeaker system and took turns ad-libbing about the scenes shown on the movie screen. An old (nearing sixty) socialist like Davenport—Dave—knew how to give a Marxian talk on housing without once using Marxian jargon. How we enjoyed telling each other about the many times we gave soapbox socialist talks and received nothing for our efforts. "Now we get paid for talking to workers, but if we so much as mentioned the word 'socialism,' the union officers would throw us out," mused Dave. The park was in a Polish neighborhood, our audience was composed largely of young Poles, and during the discussion period they invariably baited us: "We can't find jobs because you guys in the union put up seniority fences to keep us out!" Then Dave and I launched into a discussion on "Why Unemployment."

Dave and I used to brag that we could use just about any film to "broaden the social vision of workers." We called it workers' education, but where do you draw the line between education and indoctrination? When I asked Dave that question, he replied: "If you have a political line to sell and you twist the truth to fit that line—that's indoctrination. When you tell workers the truth about the things that affect their lives—that's education." I persuaded the local officers to purchase a movie projector and screen, and thereafter films became my favorite education tool to get over my message. One example will suffice. From the public library, I obtained an excellent film titled *Pasteur*, which depicts not only the scientific experiments conducted by that genius, but also the way in which the medical bureaucracy of his day tried to discredit his theories. After showing the film, I conducted a discussion about bureaucracy, beginning with the American Medical Association and ending with the growth of bureaucracy in unions. I quoted passages from Michel's *Political Parties* and suggested that unionists interested in building a labor library would do well to order a copy and read it. Nearly everyone in the class ordered a copy.

A union education department is a coveted prize for every organized political or religious group seeking to indoctrinate union members. And if a member of one group is in charge of the education department, he soon finds himself harassed by members of other groups. I know that the ACTU instructed its members in the Dodge local to attend my classes and "report what goes on there." I guess they feared I might be teaching *Das Kapital*. But my worst enemies were the Stalinists, who tried in every way to have me fired. They and their supporters controlled the local's executive board and voted on two occasions to discharge me on grounds that "there are members in Local 3 capable of educating the members of Local 3." But when their recommendation came before the membership meeting, it was overwhelmingly defeated; the shop stewards were solidly behind me.

Racist Tactic Fails

In 1939 the Dodge plant was shut down by a strike. This time I had an opportunity to learn how strikes were conducted, not merely as an observer, but as a direct participant. I marched in the picket lines, helped to put out publicity, scheduled special education sessions dealing with strike issues, sat in strategy meetings, and coordinated the work of the various strike committees in cooperation with Pat Quinn, then president of Local 3.

Pat's militant labor career began in the 1916 Irish Rebellion, and he was at his best when he was "fightin' the bloody company." In those days, the auto barons still believed the "union is not here to stay" and that a disastrous strike could wreck the UAW. Dodge officials tried to launch a successful back-to-work movement and they resorted to the racist tactic of pitting blacks against whites. One day we learned that on the following morning a large contingent of blacks would be escorted through the back gate of the Dodge plant by mounted police.

Never will I forget that morning! Strikers lined the sidewalk across from the plant's back entrance. I was standing on the roof of a garage with Pat Quinn and the other Local 3 officers. Also on the roof was a well-known pro-labor Negro minister, whose name I have forgotten. He appealed to the blacks not to act as strikebreakers. As the men marched down the street, flanked by mounted police, the minister made an eloquent plea: "Don't let the company use you to break this strike." He explained why Dodge workers were striking and urged the black workers to help the strikers and "not stab them in the back." At the same time, Pat Quinn and other officers called on the strikers to exercise self-restraint: "The company and the police are deliberately trying to provoke violence; racial violence would kill this strike and set the entire UAW back for years." There was no violence. The Negroes went into the plant, but most of them did not stay, and the back-to-work attempt flopped. For the second time in a little over two years, Dodge management surrendered to the UAW.

Marriage

In April 1939 I married Mary Koenig. I was instantly attracted to her when that small, slender blonde showed me the room which I promptly rented on East Grand Boulevard near Hamtramck. Mary lived with her mother, who rented out rooms upstairs, and her sister Olga, who was employed by the First National Bank. Mary did not have the stamina to hold down a full-time job after a long siege with tuberculosis, which she contracted while working in her brother's hospital in Hamtramck and which became so advanced that only major surgery could save her life. A young doctor took a fancy to Mary when she was convalescing in the sanatorium and influenced her to read "good books." She said, "He started me off with Darwin's *Origin of Species* and told me to mark the passages which I did not understand so that he could explain them for me." She told me that the books he recommended gave her "a whole new way of looking at things."

Mary was the direct opposite of Olga. I always marveled that two sisters who were so close and so fond of one another could be poles apart in their social attitudes. Mary's kind, gentle, sensitive nature instinctively made her recoil from expressions of racial hatred. I can still see the pained look that came over her face when Olga would rail against "those dirty niggers!" Mary often said to me: "Why don't you talk things over with Olga? Surely you can change her views about Negroes." I tried; God how I tried! Once I asked Olga to read an excellent pamphlet on the subject of race that I had distributed in my union classes. By means of visual aids and concrete examples the author explained the origin of racial characteristics, the different types of blood regardless of race, the appearance of dominant and recessive features, and so on. "After you read this pamphlet I'd like to discuss it with you," I told Olga. She never opened it.

During the years we lived in that house on East Grand Boulevard, I had a good opportunity to learn why so many white lower-middle-class people acquire such ineradicable prejudices, especially if they own homes. For years Olga slaved in banks to meet the mortgage payments on that home; to her it represented years of working, saving, and scrimping. Not only the mortgage, but repairs and improvements had to be paid for year after year. That house was Olga's stake, her nest egg, her source of security. Every petty home owner in a big city seems to be convinced that "property values slump when niggers move in the neighborhood!" There were some black families living on streets near Olga's house, and she dreaded the day when they might move closer to her, might even—God forbid—move next door! She could reel off all the hoary clichés: "Niggers are lazy, shiftless, destructive—why, just drive through the nigger sections of the city and look at the shacks they live in; once those were nice, painted homes, with nice lawns, now they are run down, unpainted, the grass is gone, and there is garbage in front of the porch. . . . " After trying over a long period and in every conceivable way to make Olga see the senselessness of her rabid prejudice, I finally told Mary: "She's a hopeless case. If she doesn't belong to the Ku Klux Klan, she's cheating them out of dues."

Mary died in 1960. Her death was a severe blow to me. During our twenty-one years of married life we had our quota of ups and downs. I could always depend on her to lend moral support when things got rough for me in the union. The humanist currents of democratic socialism appealed to her, but she never joined the Socialist Party, saying, "When you belong to a political party you are not always free to think the way you want to; every party has a line." But she always accompanied me to SP meetings and social events, and she got along well with party members; they all liked Mary. She and I had compatible interests; we went to concerts, stage plays, lectures, and took short trips during my summer vacation. Most of all we enjoyed our attractive cottage in Lexington Heights. In public we were never demonstrative in our affection for one another, but we felt it deeply. Mary was a rational person and possessed the kind of intelligence that John Dewey equated with sound, down-to-earth common sense. Her intuitive ability to size up people never ceased to amaze me. I'll never forget how correctly she called the shots in 1958 when I was among those in the Socialist Party who supported the move for unity with the Independent Socialist League (ISL), the small group of reformed Trotskyites led by Max Shachtman. I incurred the wrath of most SP members in Detroit for my efforts on behalf of unity. Mary was furious. She said I should take the lead in opposing such unity, not favor it.

"You are so naive, real gullible at times. The ISL people are not to be trusted. If unity takes place they will dominate the SP and either change its course or ruin it. You know the ISL is on the government's subversive list and unity will be one way to get them off the hook. Also, some of these people want to ingratiate themselves with the UAW, and they feel that as members of the SP they will be more readily accepted. You mark my word, they are moving to the right and that's where they'll take the SP if and when they become part of it," Mary told me.

At that time I thought her prognosis was so far-fetched that I scoffed. Mary did not live long enough to see how absolutely true her prophecy turned out to be. Under ISL influence the SP pursued policies no different from those advocated by Democratic Party liberals. In Detroit most of the former Socialists dropped out of the party in disgust and many of the erstwhile ISL members wormed their way into the UAW bureaucracy. Max Shachtman and his followers outhawked the hawks in relation to the Vietnam war, and in foreign policy they became cold warriors ā la George Meany.

Mary was so right. The SP–ISL unity business became a sorry fiasco. Stan Ovshinsky, who like myself was among those who worked diligently to bring about unity, deplored his action later. He said: "In 1937 the Trotskyites around Max Shachtman ruined the SP from the left; this time they destroyed it from the right."

As months rolled by after Mary's death I decided it is not good for a man to live alone, at least not for me. I wanted a companion—and found one. Ethel is a social worker with a master's degree in social work. Her specialty is community organization. Over the years she served as director in various YWCA centers, retiree projects, housing developments, and more community agencies than I can name. At this writing she is in Washington, D.C., assigned for three months to work with the Ralph Nader group on a pension project. The purpose of the project is to expose to public view the fraudulent ways unsuspecting workers get swindled out of their pensions upon retirement. Ethel calls herself a "pragmatist," by which she means that she has "no time for theory" but only for "practical work." I sometimes think that her emphasis on "practical work" leads to mindless activity for the sake of activity. Before going to Washington she could not find employment in Albuquerque (where budgets for social services are cut to the bone), so she threw herself into the United Farm Workers boycott movement and won the praise of Cesar Chavez for a "terrific job." She has the drive of a supercharged person, and once she gets going she does not know when to slow down. She always identified with "the lower-lowers"—the blacks, Chicanos, and Indians. In 1968–69 she worked on a community project in Inkster, Michigan, a village originally settled by blacks who worked in the Ford Rouge plant. Soon after she started on that job, two black women told her, "We like you, you are for real!" That meant they could sense that Ethel wasn't being phony when she told them: "To me there is only one race, the human race." When she works with blacks or Chicanos the reserve they show toward her at first soon vanishes when they get to know her.

Ethel also finds time to work for the Gray Panthers, an

organization for the "concerned elderly," sparked by the ninety-seven-pound dynamo Margaret "Maggie" Kuhn. According to Ethel the Gray Panthers have a revolutionary mission of radicalizing old people against the Establishment and mobilizing them for constructive social change. Old people tend to be alienated from the mainstream, relegated to a life of shuffleboard and pinochle. "There's a wealth of latent talent and potential power among millions of the elderly. We of the Gray Panthers will help to mobilize that power for progressive social action," Ethel says.

Recently Ethel discovered the Movement for a New Society (MNS), a Quaker-like group centered in Philadelphia that advocates nonviolent direct action for confronting violence and injustice. An example of such nonviolent confrontation was seen a few years ago in the voyages of the sailing ship *Phoenix* to North and South Vietnam with medical supplies. Ethel is interested in the various communities within the MNS network. In some places individuals continue to live in separate houses as before but interact with each other on more levels. Other people in the MNS are sharing homes. In some places clusters of communes and individuals form a wider community of people moving in the same direction. Ethel thinks that by operating health clinics, food cooperatives, and eventually producers' cooperatives, the MNS can point the way to a democratic, humanist alternative to dog-eat-dog capitalism.

She is also exploring other kinds of communes, notably those organized on a much larger scale and patterned somewhat after the Israeli kibbutzim. She is convinced that the nuclear family is outmoded and that alternative family forms can and will be created in communes. Ethel is endowed with strong maternal instincts. Once I told her: "Every time we go to a supermarket or elsewhere in public and you see a baby in a carriage or in the mother's arms, you fuss and coo and gush over the kid. Every cell in your body cries out for a child." Ethel's father died when she was still attending school, so she took on the responsibility of looking after her mother and could not marry when still young enough to have a baby. I think she would be much happier if she could live in a commune, especially one resembling an "extended family" where children are the concern of the whole community as in the kibbutz.

7
Ford Local 600

In 1939 General Motors was forced to come to terms with the UAW when Walter Reuther, then director of the UAW's GM department, called the skilled trades workers out on strike. So GM and Chrysler were learning the hard way that the union was something they would have to live with. However, the third member of the "Big Three" still adhered to old Henry Ford's motto: "Hell will freeze over before I recognize a union!" But the drive to organize the Ford plants was gaining momentum. Nearly every UAW local in Detroit contributed in one way or another to that all-out organizing drive. I always accompanied the group of Dodge workers when they drove to the huge River Rouge Ford complex to pass out organizing leaflets. And when the Ford strike occurred in April 1941, I again had occasion to witness how Ford, like Chrysler two years earlier, hoped to use Negroes to break the strike—and how the attempt failed. When Ford capitulated and signed an agreement with the UAW, Ford Local 600 was faced with the monumental task of setting up an administrative structure and a grievance procedure system.

The Rouge complex was composed of seventeen buildings or "units," and workers in every unit elected departmental committeemen to handle grievances. But most committeemen, and certainly all foremen, had no previous experience in handling grievances, which hardly made for smooth labor-management relations; some committeemen had weird notions about the nature of their duties. Thus in one department of the motor building, the workers chose as their committeeman a man who had done an outstanding job as picket captain during the stike. When he was elected committeeman, he walked over to the foreman, pointed to his shiny committeeman's button, and exclaimed: "Do you see this?" The foreman replied, "Ah yes, you are the new committeeman; congratulations." The committeeman snapped: "Congratulations, hell. I'm running this department now—you scram to hell out of here!" It soon dawned on Dick Leonard, UAW Ford director, that an education program was urgently

needed to train committeemen, and he asked me if I would be interested
in becoming education director of Local 600—the largest union local in
the world, with 60,000 members, the vast majority of whom were green
to unionism! What a challenge to an education director! So in August
1941, I resigned from Dodge Local 3 and began my duties in the large
Ford local. I didn't know what I was getting myself in for, but I was soon
to find out.

"Concentrate on training committeemen, teach them how to settle
grievances," Dick Leonard told me. I proceeded accordingly and soon
discovered how the Ford grievance representation system operated.
When I worked in the Dodge local, the chief steward represented a
relatively small number of workers so his constituents could readily
contact him when they needed his help. In the Ford plants the
committeemen were designated to process grievances and the ratio of
workers to committeemen was much larger than in Dodge. Ford
management was shrewd enough to grant the union plenty of leeway: a
union shop, dues check off, and "the fruits of office" to committeemen.
The committeemen were favored with offices, telephones, and "all the
time they needed to handle grievances." Mike Magee, a conscientious
unionist, socialist, and enthusiastic supporter of labor education,
reported how committeemen functioned in the Ford building where he
worked:

We can never find our committeeman when we need him. There seems
to be an agreement between the foreman and the committeeman: the
committeeman does not press the foreman too much about settling
grievances and the foreman gives the committeeman a free hand, even
gives him permission to leave the plant on the pretext of "union
business." Hell, the business of a committeeman should be to look after
our grievances in the shop and not roam around on the outside. In our
Ford setup, union-management relations contain the seeds of semi-
company unionism.

Mike urged committeemen: "Don't allow the company to buy you off
with favors. If supervision won't settle grievances within a reasonable
time—then tell the workers to slow down!"

In the summer of 1941 the more militant committeemen could get
results by urging such "power on the job." But all this changed after
Pearl Harbor. In an article printed 17 August 1942 in the *New Republic* I
wrote:

Despite the fact that a substantial number of committeemen had learned correct procedure for handling grievances, they found it more difficult to obtain favorable adjustments after Pearl Harbor. Increasingly committeemen complain that no matter how legitimate the grievance and how correct the procedure followed, the foremen and superintendents simply refuse to settle them. "The trouble is that the bosses are taking advantage of the war and are thumbing their noses at us," bitterly complained a committeeman. His complaint was borne out by replies to a questionnaire sent out by the Education Department to determine if foremen were using the (war) emergency to circumvent the provisions of the contract. Of the hundred questionnaires returned, forty-eight contained answers similar to the following:

Has the foreman or superintendent ever told you that collective bargaining doesn't mean anything, now that our country is at war?

Yes, he says we should concentrate on the war and not so much on grievance procedure. In fact, he told me I should be docked for talking to him.

No-Strike Pledge

John Honos was a very perceptive UAW member whose union background began in 1933 and whose history I taped in 1968. I asked him: "You described how stewards once had real power at the shop level. Why do you think they lost their power, and when did this happen?" He answered:

The war did it. Yes, the war killed it. In 1942 the UAW gave up the right to strike. What power does a union have when it gives up the right to strike, even gives up the right to threaten to strike? No sooner did we surrender the strike weapon than the employers gave us a hard time. Grievance procedure became a joke. At each step of the procedure, supervision would answer with a flat NO. When the company and the union agreed to set up a so-called impartial umpire system, we stewards became mere referral agents. The union contract got larger and more complicated, union procedure became more legal, grievances got channeled right up to the international union and finally to the umpire. It became more and more difficult to settle grievances on the job; now an outside party settled them. Half the umpire's salary was paid by the union and half by the company. It seemed to us workers that he favored the company more than he favored the union. He acted like a man walking a tightrope, leaning first to one side and then to the other. How in hell could grievances get settled on their merits under a system like that?

The no-strike pledge! Some labor scholar should do a documented study about the way in which auto workers responded to that "patriotic pledge." I know how Ford workers responded during the time I served as education director in Local 600. They responded by walking off their jobs, by wildcatting. How many times did I hear UAW President R.J. Thomas plead, cajole, threaten, and bawl out wildcatters in Local 600: "My Gawd, fellows, there's a war on! When you shut down your department, other departments can't operate for lack of parts, so you are hurting the war effort! Go back to work and let your union officers take up your grievances with management!" Then some committeeman would shout: "But the damn company won't settle grievances. You don't work in the plant; you don't know what in hell goes on in there. You say follow procedure, follow procedure—why don't you tell supervision to follow procedure?" Over and over, I witnessed that performance, with variations of the same theme.

During the war, the union was increasingly becoming a disciplinary agency over the workers. The international union and management cooperated to get out war production, and to prevent interruptions of production. The International is the UAW power center, housed in Detroit's Solidarity House, where the president and other international officials, assisted by their staff members, operate. The local unions are subordinate bodies whose by-laws and policies must conform to the international constitution and rulings of the International Executive Board. The International has the power to put a local under receivership if it persists in opposing international policy. One time when he was particularly angry with a group of press steel workers who wildcatted, Thomas stormed and berated them for "letting down your country in this hour of crisis" and demanded that they return to work immediately. While all of this was taking place, Bill Taylor, Dick Leonard's assistant, was sitting in a small side room, holding the phone so that one of the Ford officials at the other end of the line could hear how the UAW president was ordering the workers back on their jobs.

Local 600 was honeycombed with Stalinists and their fellow travelers. During the war, when the CP still proclaimed that "communism is twentieth-century Americanism," many workers became camp followers. CP influence was so strong that a *Detroit News* reporter told me: "The Communists organized Ford Local 600." That claim was nonsense, of course, but no one should underestimate the contributions made by the Stalinists in the drive to organize the Ford Rouge plant. In their ranks were some of the most able unionists I ever met, such as foxy old Bill McKie, an uncanny Scot with years of experience in union and radical activity. He was a master of infusing the party line in his trade union work, and he soon set his sights on our education department.

I learned that "Old Bill" called a meeting of Communist Party members in his home to plan ways to influence our education program. He maneuvered to have two of his comrades appointed to the education committee and instructed them to attend every class, lecture, and forum meeting. I always felt that education should be neutral: "The education department is financed by a percentage of dues money paid by all members of the union, therefore it should not be used to further the aims of any one group. The director of education should teach unionism, not factionalism." When I told this to Bill McKie, he said I was like an ivory tower professor (his contempt for professors was scathing): "You are like a piano player in a whore house that don't know what's going on!" Then he prophesied: ". . . sooner or later either the Reuther gang or the Addes side will be in full control of the UAW. And when that happens the international education department will be used to sell UAW policy to the membership. We're in this fight to see that our side wins and we can set policy."

I remember telling Frank Winn (then editor of *Ford Facts* and later appointed by Walter Reuther to head the UAW International publicity department): "Only a person who has been on the receiving end of their fire can really appreciate how vicious Stalinists can be toward their opponents." Winn, who was also the victim of their sniping, agreed. He became incensed when the local's executive board hired Fred Sweet to act as the "coordinator" of administrative departments. Winn and I suspected that the Communist Party members persuaded the local's top officers to hire Sweet so he could act as watchdog over *Ford Facts* and the education department. Frank and I also suspected that Sweet, a top-notch labor journalist, wanted to get full control of *Ford Facts* and use it as a propaganda medium. Winn quit the Ford local in 1943. I followed the advice of Reuther supporters in the factional fight: "Hang on as long as you can, for the moment you leave, the Commies will take over the education department." Here is how the *Ford Unionist*, a small paper issued by the anti-Stalinist forces in Local 600, summed up my running battle with the Communists in that local:

Marquart Was Victim of Political Intrigue

In the fall of 1941 Frank Marquart began his duties as Educational Director of Ford Local 600. He was asked by Richard T. Leonard, National UAW-CIO Ford Director, and the Local's Executive Board to concentrate on the education of committeemen, key members in the shop.

The response of committeemen to the classes exceeded all expectations. In the Oct. 10, 1941, issue of "Ford Facts" is a picture of a class, with this explanation:

"Anybody that says Ford workers aren't interested in union education is talking through his hat. Here are part of the midnight shift committeemen who last week answered Education Director Frank Marquart's first call for classes. More than 150 showed up in this group alone. They and others will study the technique of collective bargaining, handling grievances, how to run meetings, public speaking, etc. under the direction of competent teachers."

Sought Cooperation of All

Plainly, directing the educational work for such a large and newly organized local was going to be a big job, and Marquart sought the cooperation of all who were willing to help.

While Marquart devoted most of his time to grievance classes and materials, outside people were brought in to help in the work of mass education. Workers Service furnished a full-time librarian, a movie and recording machine specialist, and three women to assist in preparing mimeographed and printed literature for distribution at all meetings.

Help also came from within Local 600 itself. Percy Llewellyn and other Executive Board members often led discussions at classes. Frank Winn helped to form the Ford Workers Chorus.

No Burning of Books

Anyone who had anything to offer was called upon, regardless of political alignments. For the first year or so the Communist Party members in the Local and their followers cooperated without trying to impose their "line."

Included on the Educational Advisory Committee in those days were Paul Boatin, Robert Lieberman and Bill McKie. Often they submitted valuable recommendations, which were promptly accepted and appreciated.

The first sharp difference over policy in the Education Department arose in the fall of 1942, when two members of the Advisory Educational Committee asked the Director to withdraw from the shelves of the Local's library the book entitled "Out of the Night."

This the Educational Director refused to do, declaring that so long as he had charge of the department, there would be no book burning campaign in Local 600. He volunteered to appear with the two members before the Executive Board to thresh out the issue. They promptly dropped the matter.

Soviet Pamphlet

Several months later a Communist Party liner proposed that the Education Department order for wide distribution copies of the pamphlet purporting to explain the nature of Soviet trade unions. After carefully reading through the pamphlet, the Director refused to comply with the recommendation on the grounds that the pamphlet was grossly misleading.

He contended that, contrary to the pamphlet, Russia has no free and independent trade unions. What passes for trade unions in that country are simply organs of the government, national compulsory bodies whose officials are not elected by the membership, but appointed by the state.

Furthermore, argued the Education Director, Russian unions, unlike our own, do not engage primarily in the task of protecting and promoting living standards and working conditions. Rather, they function as glorified committees to raise labor productivity, instituting such means as incentives and the speed up or "socialist competition." Marquart offered to debate the question as an educational feature before a local meeting. The subject was dropped and never raised again. (Incidentally, the challenge to debate the proposition still stands . . .)

Russia Enters War—Party Line Changes

When the Party liners began to clamor more and more for the "Second Front" the Education Department met with increasing opposition. One evening, Bill McKie was invited to speak before the Educational Flying Squad on the role of unions in wartime. His typewritten speech was taken word for word from sections of the booklet written by Earl Browder, where he developed the Communist theory that the entire economy must be geared to war needs and unions should suspend for the duration their customary activities relative to improving working conditions.

Squad members took issue with McKie on many points, much to his chagrin. Thereafter McKie confined his educational activities to doing a "hatchet" job on the director.

Others Attack Flying Squad

Nor was he the only one. The Party boys really went to town in every building where they had members. They attacked the Flying Squad—naturally, since they could not steer it in the direction of their "line."

The Educational Department's emphasis on grievance procedure irked them. "We have a war to win, forget about grievance procedure," was their motto. They stressed mass education to the exclusion of group discussions and class room work.

Actually the Education Department had a full-time assistant, Albert Tracey, who rode from unit meeting to meeting, showing movies and distributing the latest leaflets. But this was not the sort of mass education the Communists wanted. By mass education they meant indoctrination of their "Second Front" slogans and their "give-up-everything-for-the-war" theories.

Story of Erlich and Alter

The peak of their animosity was reached when the Educational Director sent to the General Council members a copy of the "Michigan CIO News" containing the true story of Erlich and Alter, the two Polish socialists who were executed in Russia because they refused to act as puppets for the Soviet Union's designs on Poland.

The paper was mailed to Council members because the Party boys first raised the Erlich and Alter issue in the form of a resolution presented at the Council. According to the CP view, Erlich and Alter were aiders and abettors of fascism and anyone who presented any other version, even though supported by documentary evidence, was guilty of playing the fascist game.

If before this incident the Education director was objectionable to the Communists and their supporters, he was downright poison now. At every one of their local faction meetings they raised the cry: "Marquart must go!"

The Stalinists are not only persistent—they are also past masters in the art of political maneuvering. Knowing that they were not influential enough to have Marquart removed by the executive board or the general council at that time, they resorted to another method—a method which finally resulted in his removal.

8
Dead-End Kids

I no sooner got fired from Local 600 than I got hired by Briggs Local 212 (August 1944). Every non-Stalinist radical in Detroit envied me for my good fortune in becoming the education director of Local 212, because in those days Local 212 had a reputation for being the most militant local in the UAW. Its members were known as the "dead-end kids." Billie Friedland, a member of the Workers Party, told me: "So, now you are working for Emil Mazey's local! Boy, are you lucky!" In those days Local 212 was identified with the name of Emil Mazey, and Mazey personified militancy (Murray Kempton in one of his books called Mazey "the perennial picket captain"). In 1944, Local 212 was not only the most militant local in the UAW, but also the most independent local— independent in the sense that it was controlled by the membership and often acted in defiance of the international officers and executive board. The local's official organ, the *Voice of Local 212*, conducted a steady campaign against the no-strike pledge and other international UAW policies with which the local disagreed. When Mazey was drafted into the Army, Local 212 continued his militant policies.

It was no accident that Local 212 became so militant in its early period. Students of the labor movement have observed that the temper of a union reflects the temper of management. Briggs Manufacturing Company had a long history of brutal speedup, low wages, and vicious anti-unionism. The company's get-tough-with-the-union policy was at its height when Mazey was president of Local 212. The hard-boiled supervisors, who were conditioned over the years to drive workers like slaves, could not get over their habits just because a contract was signed with the union. Local 212 had to "educate" the foremen. Negotiating grievances was a tough business in those days, and Mazey was equal to the task. Professor Edward W. McFarland of Wayne State University once told me about the time he was engaged to arbitrate a dispute between Local 212 and Briggs management. As McFarland walked into the conference room where Mazey and his plant committee were meeting with company representatives, Mazey turned to

McFarland and told him in blunt terms: "You can't represent us; you are not a worker!" McFarland said: "Mazey's crack infuriated me, but actually I had to admit to myself that he was right."

Mazey had a knack for picking people with leadership abilities; he surrounded himself with a group of "young Turks" and built a strong political machine in his local. He was idolized by his youthful followers because, as one of them put it: "Emil never asks any of us to do anything that he himself is not prepared to do—he is always in front of the firing line." Local 212 organized a "flying squadron," whose members wore colored shirts and gained the reputation for being "tough hombres." Allan Strachan, then a member of the SP and also a member of the CIO Wayne County Council, took a dim view of the squad's tactics and mode of dress: "They look and act like storm troopers!" The squad was tough. On the picket line, squad members were ready to fight cops at the least provocation. Under Mazey's guidance, Local 212 could always be counted on in the fight against the Martin-Lovestone group and, after Martin faded out of the UAW picture, against the Addes-CP combination.

Those were the days when there was considerable local autonomy in the UAW. Mazey simply thumbed his nose at the international union administration when it tried to dictate policy to the local. And later, when R.J. Thomas headed the UAW and the Addes-controlled international executive board attempted to censor the Local 212 section of the United Auto Workers monthly paper, Mazey and his local executive board told the International to go to hell. Local 212 put out its own paper, the *Voice of Local 212*, which, of course, followed a militant line. Every issue called for a labor party, since Mazey was the strongest advocate of a labor party in that period of the UAW. During 1940, Mazey and his followers in Local 212 supported Norman Thomas for president. This almost caused fight after fight in the shop when ardent FDR supporters threatened to tear Thomas's buttons from the shirts of those who were wearing them. But no one among the FDR worshippers was rash enough to invite an encounter with the local's flying squad, and so no buttons were torn off.

The active core of Local 212 consisted of the young, militant secondary leaders in the shop—the line stewards, chief stewards, and committeemen in the Briggs plants. I could mention at least two dozen of these people by name. The Briggs local once had by far the best steward system of any local in the UAW. This was because Briggs

Company was a supplier plant and therefore vulnerable to union pressure. When, for example, Chrysler gave Briggs a fat contract for auto bodies, Chrysler expected and demanded that those bodies be delivered according to agreement. Consequently, Briggs was forced to yield concessions to the union which General Motors, Chrysler, and Ford never yielded. Even line stewards received recognition in the Briggs contract. (In the 1950s, when Chrysler bought out the Briggs body plants and equipment, Chrysler management lost no time trimming down the steward system and tightening discipline over the work force.)

The key men in the steward body were Mazey supporters; they were also the key men in the Mazey local political machine and in the flying squad. The secondary leaders were deeply influenced by the clever, shrewd, and self-educated young socialist Billie Lamson, when he was the local's first eduction director (he was later killed in World War II). "When I first attended Lamson's classes, I didn't even know what the letters 'CIO' stood for, but thanks to him, I soon became a militant unionist," Ken Morris (now a UAW international regional director) told me. When Mazey was drafted into the armed forces, his supporters carried on the fight against the no-strike pledge, against the incentive system which the Communists sought to saddle on the UAW, against the unfair rulings of the War Labor Board, against the company which tried in every way to take advantage of the wartime labor regulations to weaken the union, against the UAW's so-called "equality of sacrifice program."

Slowdowns and walkouts by Briggs workers were frequent during the war years, and militant unionists were singled out and fired. But the firings only provoked more walkouts. At one period during the war, labor trouble in Briggs made headlines, not only in the Detroit dailies but also in a New York City daily called *PM*, which sent a reporter to Detroit to investigate. The *PM* story was factual and interspersed with quotations by Briggs production workers, Local 212 officers, committeemen, chief stewards, and myself, as the local's education director.

If Local 212 gave management trouble, it also became a thorn in the side of the international UAW. I will never forget that memorable day at the 1944 UAW Convention when President R.J. Thomas spoke to the delegates, calling on them to remember there was a war on, that all good union members must support their country in the hour of its greatest need, and that opponents of the no-strike pledge and rebellious workers who precipitated walkouts in plants producing war materials were letting their country down. In the midst of his patriotic harangue, the delegation seated at the Local 212 tables pulled out little American flags and began to wave them with one hand while wiping away mock tears with the other hand. Thomas became furious. Some of the Communists and their fellow travelers shouted: "Throw them out of the convention!" Other delegates booed the Local 212 group, but the majority of the delegates and the gallery spectators merely laughed.

I could cite many other incidents to indicate the spirit that prevailed among Local 212 members, especially secondary leaders, in those early days. The *Daily Worker* carried front-page editorials denouncing Local 212 leaders as Trotskyites, which they definitely were not, though some members of that party were active in the local. Those members tried to exploit the militancy for their party's ends, but they did not cause the disturbances and at no time did they control the policy-making machinery of the local. That militancy was simply the product of a series of factors: the tough anti-union policy of management, the militant tradition bequeathed by Mazey, and War Labor Board policies.

Terror

Briggs officials gave a new twist to their labor policies when they made a deal with a Detroit scrap iron dealer who agreed to "take care of union trouble makers" in return for a profitable scrap iron contract. In his book *Detroit, City of Race and Class Violence*, B.J. Widick gives a graphic account of that tie-up between Briggs management and racketeers. Of the six Local 212 members beaten up by goons as a result of that scrap iron bargain, two of them—Genora Dollinger and Ken Morris—were nearly killed. I first met Genora when she was the wife of Kermit Johnson, one of the key leaders in the Flint sit-down strike in 1936–37. At that time the Johnsons were members of the SP and on several occasions spoke at our Branch 2 meetings about the latest developments of the Flint struggle. In his story of the Flint sit-down, Sidney Fine has this to say about Genora: "The initiative in forming the Women's Emergency Brigade as a unit of the (women's) Auxiliary was taken by twenty-three year old Genora Johnson, a tall, curly-haired and brown-eyed mother of two and the wife of the Chevrolet No. 4 strike leader, Kermit Johnson." When I became education director of Local 212, Genora (then the wife of Sol Dollinger) was a chief steward in the Briggs Mack Avenue plant and the editor of *On Guard*, a monthly steward bulletin that exposed supervision's violations of the union contract and bristled with pointed attacks against foremen whom Genora accused of union-busting tactics. A worker in her department told me: "The foremen hate Genora's guts; she's not afraid to tell them off when they stall on grievances."

Early one morning I received an emergency call from Local 212's president, John Murphy, who told me to accompany him to the Detroit General Hospital, where Genora had been rushed after two goons broke into her home before dawn. One goon kept her husband covered with a gun while the other goon beat her severely with a blackjack. When Murphy and I arrived at the hospital, tears of pain trickled down her cheeks, her face was black and blue, her collarbone was broken, and the doctor told me: "They could have killed that girl; you should see how her body is bruised all over!"

The beatings grew worse with each successive victim. Ken Morris, then Local 212 recording secretary, was slugged when he stepped out of his car in front of his apartment one evening. So critically was Ken beaten about the head and face that doctors feared brain injury, but fortunately he recovered fully. I believe that every key member of Local 212 wondered if he would be the next victim. As editor of the *Voice of Local 212*, I wrote editorials warning the "power behind the beatings" that the members of Local 212 would not stand by idly and see their fellow unionists terrorized and beaten half to death. I had uneasy feelings every time I drove my car in the parking lot at night and then walked across the street to my home.

Careerism

When I started to work for Local 212, it was a proud, independent, fighting local which never hesitated to take on the international union when the latter tried to dictate policy. What has become of all those bold spirits who formed the backbone of the local in its heyday? Some were fired for their militancy and found jobs in other fields. Some have faded out of the picture and no one in Local 212 knows where they are. More than a score of those former militants have been placed on the international union payroll and their new mode of life has turned them into "porkchoppers"—that is, into organization men for the UAW hierarchy. There is something corrupt about the making of a porkchopper, and the corrupting influence comes from the top down, not from the bottom up.

Let me describe a not untypical example. A man I will call X was one of the most able, conscientious, and militant secondary leaders at the shop level. He won the respect of the workers in his shop district and they always supported him at election time. Hence over the years he served successively as line steward, chief steward, and committeeman. In the early days he was firmly convinced that a conflict of interest existed between the local and the international union and he always stood four-square on the side of the local union. In the presence of fellow workers he often denounced the International's officers and representatives for their wishy-washy attitude when negotiating speedup grievances which the local plant committee could not settle because management remained adamant. He was active in his local union faction, attended membership meetings regularly, and became an able floor leader.

He eventually was elected a delegate to the international UAW constitutional convention, where he mingled with international representatives who once worked in the shop like himself but who now followed an altogether different life style. He knew that those representatives earned at least two and one-half times as much money as he did; they did not have to submit to factory discipline, breathe in factory pollution, eat indigestible food from factory lunch wagons, and they always wore white-collar clothes instead of work clothes. He felt that he too was fully qualified to perform the duties of an international representative.

At home his wife often reminded him of this fact. Her complaint went something like this: "Nobody else works as hard as you do for that union. You attend every meeting, campaign in every election, do a good job as committeeman—but where does all this get you? You're still in the shop. Look at Y. He got out of the shop, he now works in the International and brings home a much bigger pay check than you do. . . ."

How often have I heard active shop leaders tell me about receiving such sermons from their wives! So X decided to "play his cards right." He knew that he was in the right faction—the faction that always supported the international hierarchy. When attending union meetings, X overlooked no opportunity to speak in support of the policies of that hierarchy. And he bitterly attacked anyone from the opposing faction who spoke against such policies. He knew that the more he proved his loyalty to the machine, the better his chances of getting on the international payroll. He remembered how convention delegates from his local were rewarded for betraying their local's instructions. At a pre-convention local union meeting, the membership voted to instruct their delegates to vote against the resolution calling for a dues increase. But when the delegates went to the convention their regional director met with a number of them and persuaded them to ignore their local's instructions and vote in favor of the dues increase. One of those delegates was an able committeeman, highly regarded by his constituents, but when they heard how he violated the local's instructions they immediately called a meeting and voted to recall him. Soon after this happened he was appointed to the international UAW staff as a representative.

X also knew that if he wanted "to get ahead" he must never voice opposition to any UAW policy, no matter how much he personally disagreed with it. Thus in 1958, when Walter Reuther publicly announced that the UAW would bargain with auto companies for a profit-sharing plan, the militant unionists in the UAW denounced the profit-sharing measure as a phony issue. "The UAW leadership proposes profit-sharing in lieu of the shorter work week because they haven't got the guts to fight for shorter hours," said a Local 212 militant.

Privately, X agreed with him, but at a membership meeting he made an eloquent speech in favor of profit-sharing. For such loyalty to the hierarchy, X was awarded a job on the international union staff. Local union officers were similarly rewarded if they proved their "reliability" to the International. Their reliability was measured by the degree to which they "kept the ranks in line"—which means getting wildcatters back to work as soon as possible, "selling" UAW policy to the membership, and, above all else, beating down any opposition in the local that might be a threat to the hierarchy. I have found that in many cases these representatives come to identify with the international union establishment; they convince themselves that "the top leadership is more progressive than the rank and file," and they rationalize and defend the aims and policies that come down from above. Their outlook changes with their life style.

Hierarchy

International staff people are the liaison men between the international union and the local union. Because of this liaison relationship any opposition group has a slim chance of winning top posts in a local election. The way the International maintains its hold over loyal local administrations would make a study which academic experts in labor affairs ought to undertake sometime. Consider what chance a local opposition group would have running a slate of candidates for important local positions in the face of the overwhelming resources which the ruling apparatus in the International can bring to bear during an election campaign. Such opposition has to fight the combined resources of the local officials and the International. What are those resources? Here is a partial list of some of the more important items—a list that virtually adds up to a formula for perpetuating the rule of the union hierarchy:

1. The local officers and their political machine have ready access to reams of mimeograph paper, mimeograph machines, and the skilled office help who get paid to work long hours of overtime to put out campaign literature.

2. International publicity experts are assigned to write campaign literature on behalf of the local's incumbents.

3. The local officers schedule a party for retirees a few weeks before the local election. The retirees are treated to food, refreshments, and the opportunity to meet old friends, especially those now on the international staff. The retirees also listen to speeches by former officers of the local, now on the international staff, and by local top officers. The speeches praise the local administration and urge the retirees to vote for the incumbents in the forthcoming election and assure "good, progressive, militant unionism."

4. On election day, local officers and international staff people use their cars to bring retirees to the local to vote and then take them back home.

5. The local's official publication is monopolized by the incumbent officers in cooperation with the international regional director and his staff. I know all about this. As editor of the *Voice of Local 212*, I was under strict instructions by the local officers not to print anything submitted by members of the "opposition group." And when the local was in the midst of an election campaign, I was not trusted to put out the

paper myself. I had to bring all my copy to the regional office in Solidarity House, where the regional director and two of his staff members, plus the president of Local 212, would make up the paper. The *Voice* was never the voice of the membership, but the voice of the ruling clique. (More bureaucratic methods are discussed in chapter 10.)

Against such odds, what chance do the candidates of an opposition group have to win an election? They are lucky if they can raise enough money to print a single issue of a campaign newspaper. After repeated defeats, members of the opposition get discouraged. In Local 212, the incumbents belonged to the "Green Slate," which was also called the "Reuther-Mazey Slate," and the opposition belonged to the "White Slate." When Tony Czerwinski, long a leader of the White Slate group, finally jumped on the bandwagon by going over to the Green Slate, he gave me this reason for the switch: "I banged my head against the stone wall long enough. The Green Slaters have all the advantages on their side; they are part of the Reuther-Mazey machine and that machine is too powerful to buck." Tony didn't tell me he was promised a job in Solidarity House if he joined the Green Slate, but when he was put on the international payroll, I drew my own conclusions. Other White Slaters switched sides, and when I kidded one of them about this, he laughed: "Hell, if you can't beat them, join them."

In campaign literature distributed among the membership during election time, the opposition always denounces the incumbents for the things they should have done but did not do—and then lists its own "program" of promises for a new and better deal. But from what I know about union local politics, I can testify that when the "outs" get "in," their fine promises never materialize, especially their promise to win speedy settlements on major grievances. Those who fill top offices in a union local soon discover that they must operate within two frameworks—the administrative framework of the local as defined by the union constitution and bylaws, and the labor-management framework as structured by the labor contract. In the early days of the UAW, a local union administrator could set the local's course in a progressive, militant direction, as Emil Mazey did during his presidency of Local 212. But no Mazey could do this today. When he was a member of Local 212, Ernest Mazey, Emil's brother, fought valiantly against the steady bureaucratic drift of the local, but he and the minority who supported him waged a losing battle. Eventually Ernest gave up the hopeless fight and devoted his talents to the American Civil Liberties Union.

Town Hall

During an election campaign, the incumbent local officers called for teamwork in the leadership and solidarity in the ranks. "By solidarity in the ranks, they mean they want the ranks solidly behind their political machine," said a leader in the White Slate group. And like bureaucrats the world over, incumbent officers fear anything that might upset their applecart or disturb their control. A case in point was our Local 212 "Town Hall," the title I gave to our biweekly open forum, which featured lectures, debates, panel discussions, and controversial documentary films. At first the local officers approved of Town Hall, then they tried to dictate the selection of speakers. When they could not do that, they sabotaged the programs.

One time I invited Roy Reuther, director of the UAW political action department, to lecture on "Why the UAW supports Democratic Party candidates." When I learned that a French labor team was visiting Detroit, I invited them to hear Roy. The meeting was well attended; it seemed to me that every UAW radical on the East Side of Detroit was there that evening. The French workers were equipped with earphones and listened intently to Roy's lecture as it was being translated into French. They were positively entranced by the hard-hitting speeches they heard during the discussion period. I could see that Roy was getting more and more uncomfortable as one speaker after another criticized the UAW leadership for allowing the union "to become hog-tied to the Democratic Party." And he had reason to become exasperated when politically knowledgeable mavericks like B.J. Widick, Al Nash, Ernest Mazey, Erwin Baur, and other uncompromising advocates of a labor party revealed the weaknesses of the UAW's political action policies. Later the French workers marveled that "the American working class is far more class conscious than our French workers." When they were told that the radicals they heard at Town Hall were by no means representative of the American working class, they protested: "But we could see they were workers . . . they dressed in working clothes and they work in the factory!" The Local 212 officers were not favorably impressed by what took place that evening. After the meeting they hastened to assure Roy that they in no way shared the views expressed by his critics.

Political action was not the only controversial subject debated in Town Hall. Ernest Mazey and Erwin Baur debated Tom Clampitt and myself on the proposition "Should the UAW bargain for a cost-of-living or wage escalator?" At that time, the Trotskyites were the strongest advocates of wage escalation. I learned later that Leon Trotsky first raised this issue as a "transitional demand"; he theorized that the employers would not grant it, but in the course of fighting for it workers would become more radicalized. When we debated the subject in Town Hall, the UAW was opposed to the escalation principle on the ground that "what goes up, must come down." Accordingly, the local officers were opposed to our holding the debate because "it's against UAW policy!" I consulted the education committee and they agreed that "the show must go on!" Ernest Mazey and Erwin Baur are formidable debators. Clampitt and I got trounced.

Another subject was debated: "Resolved that the international UAW officers be elected by referendum." This threw the local officers into a dither. A regional director from Detroit's East Side said such a debate should not be scheduled. He argued to the effect that there were so many "backward" members in the union that Walter Reuther could conceivably be defeated in a referendum election. I interpreted this to mean that the overwhelming majority of the delegates who elect top officers at UAW conventions could always be counted on to support the Reuther machine. A well-entrenched union bureaucracy can manipulate and control convention delegates, but no such control could be exercised on the membership-at-large voting by referendum. To even suggest a referendum system for the UAW was considered disloyal by the UAW officers. But when at the conclusion of the debate I asked for a show of hands from the rank and file workers in the audience, nearly everyone favored the referendum. The next day, one of the local officers told me that under no circumstances must I raise the referendum question in the *Voice of Local 212.*

Wildcats

From the standpoint of the local officers, the most disloyal event occurred when Irving Canter (about whom more will be written later) discussed wildcat strikes in our Town Hall. From first-hand experience, he gave a concrete account of what happens in a wildcat strike. I will reconstruct the gist of his talk from memory:

Look behind a wildcat strike and you'll nearly always find a major grievance that supervision refuses to resolve. The workers involved in the grievance—a speedup, for example—refer it to their steward, who in turn refers it to the foreman, who in turn tells the steward to refer it to the next stage of the grievance procedure. And while the grievance moves step by step through this cumbersome process, the workers are expected to continue working under the aggrieved conditions. Each day when they inquire about their grievance, the steward assures them it is being processed at the higher stage of the procedure. Each day the workers become more frustrated and irked, and sooner or later some of them say to hell with it and walk off the job. The company singles out the alleged ring leaders and fires them, justifying its action by the no-strike clause in the union contract.

Now the union local faces double trouble. The local officers seek to get the discharged men back to work, but the company states flatly that it will not budge until the wildcatters return to their jobs. Sometimes this provokes more men in the shop to walk out, and the local union is confronted with a crisis. The officers call their UAW regional director, who sends one of his staff representatives to the troubled local. In the shop, discontent spreads from department to department. The workers demand that the officers get the discharged men reinstated. The officers and international UAW representative call a special meeting. The officers report that they are doing all in their power to have the men reinstated, but the company won't negotiate until the wildcatters go back to work. Tempers flare. The workers call for strike action; the international representative assures them that under the UAW contract workers are allowed to strike over bad working conditions, but first the union must exhaust all steps in the grievance procedure. Now the meeting gets out of hand; the workers boo the officers and the international UAW representative.

Under this pressure, the officers agree to call a special meeting for a strike vote; another meeting is called, a strike vote is taken, but the workers are reminded that no strike can be called unless and until authorized by the international UAW executive board. There's the rub. All the local officers, the regional director, and his staff members are on the platform. One by one, they harangue the members about the need to follow procedure, since a strike can be called only as a last resort, when all other means have failed. The people on the platform monopolize the meeting, they talk *at* the workers until they become weary. Finally, when each person on the platform has had his long say, the local president calls for comments from the members. Every time a worker takes the floor and complains about the way the company makes a mockery of procedure by stalling on grievances, he is assured by the local officers and regional director—who again engage in long harangues—that "we will do all in our power to win this case!" The members lose their patience; they get hot under the collar; they boo, jeer, and file out of the meeting in disgust. No strike gets called; the wildcatters go back to work—all except the two who were discharged.

Canter cited the number of times this kind of performance occurred in his local, and then he asked: "Is it any wonder that workers lose faith in the union? Is it any wonder that not enough members show up at union membership meetings to form a quorum?"

Canter's talk marked the beginning of the end of Town Hall. As he was walking out of the hall, one of the local officers grabbed him by the arm and warned: "Keep to hell away from this local; if you want to rabble-rouse, do it in your own local!" Erwin Baur, another Socialist, was also ordered to stay away. When I scheduled a panel discussion on "Union Ethics," it had to be canceled because the officers locked the door and we couldn't get in. The next day, I told the local president: "Look, I got the message. As far as I'm concerned, there will be no more Town Hall. You officers sabotaged it to death."

That local president was a valuable asset to the Reuther-Mazey machine, and when he ran for the post of East Side regional director, the machine saw to it that he got elected. In his winter 1972 *Dissent* article, Bernard Rosenberg wrote: "In the old days, Local 6 had an education director, since eliminated, presumably over conflict with a regional director, and not replaced thereafter." Then Rosenberg quoted a Local 6 Socialist leader as saying: "This local used to be an educational arena in which men developed. . . . We created union-mindedness and diffused it . . . people carried away a concept of dynamic unionism. No more." This passage is an apt summary of what also happened in Local 212.

Plain Talk

In addition to classes, forums, and movies, the union's monthly paper, *Voice of Local 212*, served as another educational medium. As editor, I regularly contributed a column titled "Plain Talk" and wrote to raise the social consciousness of Briggs workers. My two favorite themes were union democracy and production for use. I played those themes over and over, each time with new variations. I tried to show that wars, poverty, inequality of income, unemployment, and other such social ills are endemic to our economic and social arrangements under which goods are produced to maximize profits and not primarily to satisfy human needs. Citing the auto industry as an example, I explained that a small minority of powerful people control the commanding heights of industry. This small class determines what is to be produced, how much is to be produced, how the products are to be distributed, what prices are to be administered to assure a substantial rate of profit. Using the factual materials put out by the UAW research department, I could expose the profit-gouging nature of the private enterprise system.

I never used radical jargon but explained in plain English how "working people of hand and brain" (a phrase often used by Norman Thomas) are divorced from the control of production and are themselves treated as factors of production by those who have control over them. I argued that the working people themselves should control the means of production—that the people should control and democratically manage the economic, political, and social affairs that vitally affect their lives. And I took pains to point out that I was in no sense advocating government ownership such as prevails in Russia, which I described as state capitalism.

I stressed that there is no difference in kind, but only in degree, between the Democratic and Republican parties, since both are committed to the administration of capitalism. Typical of the kind of articles I wrote on economics is the following "Plain Talk" column:

If the auto workers were told that they spend half of their time in the shops working for themselves and the other half of the time working for their employers, they probably wouldn't believe it.

But if they will consult the report on the auto industry issued by the Federal Trade Commission, they can discover the facts for themselves. Taking the period from 1899 to 1937, the Commission showed that the workers received approximately one-half of the "value added by manufacture" during that long time.

"Value added by manufacture" does not include the value of materials or of machine depreciation. "Value added by manufacture" means the value added to the materials in the process of converting them into the finished product. During an eight-hour day, the worker adds value to the materials on which he works—whether he machines them or assembles them. Of this newly-added value he receives about one-half in the form of wages.

In other words, every time the auto workers create $16 in new value, they are paid around $8 in wages. The Federal Trade

Commission was not the only body to discover this ratio of wages to added value.

The General Motors Brief published by the UAW more than a year ago cited figures showing that every time G.M. workers are paid $1.07 in wages, the corporation takes in $1.09 in profits.

Heart of the Struggle

People are said to be exploited when they receive less than they produce. A share of what they produce is taken away from them. This is the same thing as saying that they have to work part of the time for others. In the case of the auto workers, this time which is spent working for others amounts to approximately one-half of the total labor time.

Obviously, if labor gets more of the value it produces, then capital must receive less. Or, turning the matter around, if the manufacturers get more of the total labor product, then labor will have to get along on less.

Here we come to the very heart of the struggle between capital and labor. It is to the interest of capital to get as much of the labor product as possible.

If the workers can be forced to accept lower wages, or to turn out more production for the same wages, then capital can obtain a larger share of what labor produces.

Conversely, if the workers can win higher wages, vacation with pay, shorter hours for the same pay, then the industrialists will have to be satisfied with less profits.

This conflicting interest between capital and labor accounts for the bitter struggles that have taken place over union demands for substantial gains, and this conflict between capital and labor also explains how vitally important a union is to working people.

Helpless Alone

A union is labor's defensive organization against the tendency of capital to depress living standards and working conditions in the hungry drive for more and ever more profits. To learn how true this is, one has only to compare wages in unionized industries with those of non-unionized industries.

As an individual the worker would stand helpless before the onslaught of the rich and powerfully organized manufacturers. Alone, the worker would be as helpless as a rabbit in the path of an Army tank.

Only by combining their numbers in a strong union do the workers stand a chance of resisting capital's downward push on their working standards and living conditions.

Organized in a strong union, workers can not only fight to hold what they have, but can, under favorable circumstances, win new gains. This, however, is as far as they can go by union action alone.

Through unions alone, the working people can never hope to end the system under which they are forced to labor for others. To change this system, other goals and another type of organization is needed.

With respect to trade union democracy I told workers that a union can be no better than its members. Unless the members remain vigilant, attend meetings, and consciously participate in forming policy, a clique will inevitably take over and the union will be ruled from the top down. Here in a "Plain Talk" column is an example of how I treated this theme:

Some people idealize unions, refuse to take a critical attitude toward them, and close their eyes to their faults. Unions are highly valuable organizations to working people and they cannot afford to do without them. But as institutions that have sprung up under our present capitalist society, they have acquired many unfortunate features and we would be unrealistic if we ignored them.

In this connection the article called "Democracy in the Unions" printed in *Labor and Nation* bears reading. The author, Anthony Ramuglia, points out the undemocratic character of many American unions. These unions function like big city political machines. In such unions can be found the counterparts of the Hagues, Pendergasts, Vares, Penroses, and other powerful political bosses.

"In many of our unions the democratic processes are as much a mockery as in the sectors of our nation just referred to," says Ramuglia. Then he goes on to charge that in some unions there is not even any pretense of democracy. And in general, both in the CIO and in the AFL, there is a top heaviness of concentrated power.

People serving in important posts are often merely appointed, not elected. Being appointed, they must do the bidding of those who appoint them, although they are supposed to represent the membership in their respective localities.

Not only is power concentrated at the top, but the constitutions of some unions are actual blue prints for dictatorship. In addition all sorts of political shenanigans go on in union conventions, not unlike the deals, wire pulling, and "fixing" that goes on in big political conventions.

What has brought so many unions to this pass? Sixty or seventy years ago, unions had far more local autonomy and therefore more direct democratic control by the membership. Large unions, however, require a certain amount of concentration because they are forced to deal with highly concentrated, large-scale industry. Those who want to find excuses for the existence of dictatorship practices argue that democracy and concentration cannot go together. Indeed, some go so far as to say that efficiency is impaired by democracy and a union can become efficient only if it is controlled by the officials at the top.

But a union that is marked by tight control from above and the absence of membership participation in vital affairs is a sick union. In such a union a gulf develops between the leaders and the membership. The members become apathetic, indifferent, and even cynical. The life and vigor of the organization becomes dried up.

Of all organizations, a union needs the invigorating influence of conscious participation on the part of the members. Only in this way can it be saved from bureaucratic dry rot. The workers must identify themselves with their union by taking part in its activities, conflicts, internal struggles and worries.

The question of democracy in the unions is not a moral question. The lack of democracy in unions is not to be deplored because it is ethically bad, but because it is harmful. If the workers cannot conduct their own organizations democratically and progressively, what hope is there that they will be able to pioneer beyond the day to day struggle for a few cents more an hour?

"The unions should and will be the training ground for active and alert citizenship in the nation rather than the dark caves of personal chicanery and power," writes Ramuglia.

I take this to mean that unions should be training schools to fit the workers to struggle for a higher and better way of life. Only by actual participation in the task of running their own organizations can working people develop social vision and initiative.

Libraries

In each of the three locals for which I worked I set up a library consisting of books on economic, social, political, and labor subjects. I added a shelf of fiction which included novels by Jack London, Upton Sinclair, John Steinbeck, and Emil Zola's classic about French mine workers, *Germinal*. During the earlier years of the UAW many locals invested considerable money from their education funds to build up libraries. Walter Reuther's Local 174 bought the entire library from the Brookwood Labor College after that institution folded. Although other locals did not possess such an imposing collection, they frequently boasted in their union papers about the size of their labor libraries. Those of us who were so enthusiastically engaged in setting up libraries sooner or later realized that we had greatly overestimated the extent to which workers would take out books and read them.

Actually only a handful of radicals in each local borrowed books from the union library frequently. The vast majority of the union members ignored the library. I often wrote book reviews in the union paper and urged members to "take advantage of your union library." Now and then a worker asked for a "how-to-do-it" book and if it was not in our collection I ordered it. I recall the chap in Local 600 who was determined to become an operating engineer in the power house. He read and reread every text he could obtain on the subject. Some of the volumes I ordered for him seemed to me to be highly technical, but he mastered them. The last time I saw him he was a full-fledged member of the Operating Engineers Union.

Those union local libraries fell far short of expectations. As the years passed they merely gathered dust from neglect. Often they were looted; a volume would be taken from the shelf and never returned. The best books disappeared that way. Since I left Local 212 in 1958 the composition of the UAW membership has been changing steadily; a much higher percentage consists of young workers between the ages of 20 and 30. And the ratio of blacks to whites is rising. I don't know how reader interest among auto workers would rate today.

Summer School

When I was education director of Local 212, I always spent one week teaching at the Michigan FDR-CIO Labor Center at Lakeport. The school first opened in 1946 and continued every summer until the CIO sold the property in the 1960s. In 1946–47 it was a real pleasure to teach there. I conducted the sessions on economics and brought in the best resource people I could get—Nat Weinberg, UAW research director and a top-ranking labor economist; Art Elder, tax expert; Sam Jacobs, whose pie chart lecture on the distribution of the national income never failed to provoke eager questions and discussion. To show that economics can't be understood apart from politics, I had the students debate such questions as: "Why did FDR's New Deal fail to solve large-scale unemployment from 1933 to 1940?" and "Do we need political realignment in America?" Not one time during those first two summer schools did the people in charge try in any way to interfere with the way I handled the classes. Not once did I hear the cry: "It's against CIO policy!" Repeatedly, I told the students, "These are debatable issues; you learn best in the give-and-take of controversy." Very often the controversy that began in my morning class would be resumed again at night in bull sessions. Those bull sessions, which often lasted for hours, were really think sessions, and I believe the workers learned more from them than they did from the formal classes.

In my experience, the ten years from 1937 to 1947 marked the best period of the UAW—during that period the international union was still fluid and not yet stratified. This is what George Lyons, Local 174's education director, had in mind when he told me in 1950: "I'm the education director of Walter Reuther's home local, and I'm glad the Reuther group now controls the UAW. Yet I don't think it's good when one group dominates the union. When the Reuther group and the Thomas-Addes group were fighting for power, the union locals could always count on getting quicker and better service from the International. Each side in the factional fight wanted to outdo the other side in pleasing the locals, whose support they sought. Every time I called upon the international education department or research department for materials or for some other kind of assistance, the response was quick and helpful. Now when I ask for such help, I have to wait for days before they finally come through." Then Lyons complained about something much more significant: "We no longer have the kind of democracy we once had. Our democracy is becoming more and more controlled . . . that's what we've got—controlled democracy. Here at this summer school, there is less freedom to teach. Our UAW teaching content is supervised from above. And we are getting less and less trade union education and more and more the kind of education that is tied in with local, state, and national politics. It's really not education at all, but propaganda for the Democratic Party. But you can't teach the truth about the Democratic Party—for example, the role of the Democratic Party in the south—otherwise you will catch hell from the international representatives."

George was right. I myself caught hell when I arranged to have Lewis Corey conduct two sessions in economics. At that time Corey was active in the Ohio Third Party movement. He had written some excellent pamphlets spelling out the economic program of the Third Party and distributed the pamphlets to the workers in his UAW summer school class. When the directors of the school heard about this, they nearly ran both Corey and me out of the camp. Both of us had to promise not to refer to any Third Party movement again. Later, Joseph Kowalski, UAW assistant education director, warned me, "Don't you ever bring that guy Corey to this summer school again!" I explained to Kowalski that Corey expressly told the students to read the pamphlets so they could discuss them pro and con. "The only literature that will be handed out in this camp is CIO literature—and that will be discussed pro, not con," Kowalski retorted.

Muzzled

In a letter which he wrote to me in 1964, Stoyan Menton, former director of the Michigan State University Labor Institute and long active in workers' education, gave his version of how education was muzzled at the FDR-CIO Labor Center.

What a contrast between the enthusiasm and freedom to discuss, inquire, explore, and experiment that once characterized the leadership training institute and the stiff, formalized kind of training and indoctrination that was taking place at the FDR labor camp the last time I visited there. A UAW education representative was distributing pre-cooked and pre-digested, euphemistically called "pre-tested," discussion outlines to the "teachers," along with detailed instructions of what the students were expected to regurgitate. A university official was invited to the CIO-FDR camp to observe "union democracy" in action. They were discussing some controversial issue, all outlined in a one-sided way, with one-sided fact sheets which clearly insinuated which were the "right" and "wrong" positions. During the discussion, some of the union members expressed dissenting views and were slapped down and all but read out of the union movement by the discussion leader. After that, the dissenters clammed up. My university friend agreed strongly with the union's position but felt that the issue should have been debated fully, especially since he knew that only a minority of union members present agreed with the position without reservations.

I recall an open forum I organized at the CIO-FDR when Brendan Sexton was assistant director of education. The topic for discussion was "productivity increments," which the Reuthers opposed at that time as a form of piecework. The issue was to be handled by a panel consisting of two workers in favor and two opposed and a neutral chairman. But I told the participants it was not to be a debate; therefore, they were under no obligation to stick to a position, and if they were convinced by those who started out with a different viewpoint, to feel free to admit they changed their minds. Well, as a result of the exchange between the panelists, some workers in the hall, who had been opposed to productivity increments, changed their minds from opposition to qualified support. After about five minutes, I heard Brendan Sexton scream obscenities in my ear for permitting this to happen, threatening to throw me and the whole university staff out of the camp. A few months later, Walter Reuther also changed his mind and came out for productivity increments with the same kind of provisions suggested by the roundly denounced heretics and renegades on the panel. At the next year's institute, explaining and selling the new position became one of the major targets.

While on this subject, let me tell you about the time Brendan Sexton asked me to provide a university political science professor with a pro-labor and anti-communist orientation to lead a discussion on "Labor's Stake in Foreign Policy" for a meeting of UAW international representatives. I asked the professor, who was that department's expert on European labor movements and now heads the department, to perform that role. He was as vigorous in his manner of expression as Brendan. He gave a critique of foreign policy from a pro-labor but anti-communist viewpoint. At that time, the CIO, and most especially the UAW, was supporting American foreign policy almost uncritically. Brendan and Leonard Woodcock—to the shock of the international representatives (who later told me it was about the most educationally stimulating session they ever had) and to the horror and chagrin of the professor who said that even ultra-conservative business groups he addressed never insulted him that way—interrupted and ordered him out of the room. Later Brendan told me that as far as he was concerned I was through as head of Michigan State University's workers' education program because of that professor's performance.

Menton told me that no person in the employ of a Michigan university labor institute can hold his job if he is unacceptable to the powerful UAW. That's why MSU fired him. In later years I told Menton that his getting fired was a blessing in disguise, for now he is a sociology professor in a private college and has much more freedom to teach than he would have had in UAW institutes.

With each passing year, UAW summer school education became more like political action seminars: how to conduct registration campaigns; how to talk to prospective voters in doorbell-ringing campaigns; how to operate voting machines properly; how to check the records of political candidates; how a bill gets processed in Congress; and so on. Of course there were the usual tool courses—steward training, collective bargaining, union administration, and others—but controversial issues were ruled out. When Irving Canter suggested at an evening session that we discuss how the Democratic Party is influenced by big business interests, he was howled down by the discussion leader: "What do you want to do, slander the Democratic Party!" Once I sat in a class conducted by an international UAW representative who was discussing the Democratic Party. He told the students that "there would be no UAW today if Governor Murphy had used the National Guard to break the General Motors sit-down strike." I waited to see how the students would react to that version of the Flint victory.

I didn't have long to wait. Irving Canter, one of the students in the class, berated the instructor for "sloughing over the class struggle" by completely ignoring what the sit-down strikers did in Flint. Later that day, I listened to Canter and Roy Reuther argue heatedly about the

UAW's education program. Roy insisted that the UAW was far ahead of other unions in pioneering new approaches to workers' education. Canter agreed that the UAW was ahead of other unions in experimenting with new techniques but failed to educate its members about the basic causes of war, unemployment, and so on. When Canter mentioned the "class struggle" during the argument, Roy fumed, "Don't use that kind of sectarian Marxist crap in this school!" To mention the class struggle was like waving a red cape before a bull.

Lynd's Bombshell

This brings to mind the memorable event that occurred when the famous sociologist Robert Lynd spoke at a UAW National Education Conference on the subject "Education for What?" Lynd stressed two themes: (1) workers' education is misguided when it fails to reveal the class struggle, and (2) for workers the only kind of political party that makes sense is a class party or labor party. I could see that those in charge of the school were taken aback by what Lynd had to say—the last thing they wanted to hear at that conference was a hard-hitting class struggle talk. But the radicals in the audience were delighted. I happened to be sitting behind Carl Shier (one of the UAW Local 6 stormy petrels) when Lynd spoke. Shier jumped to a point of order and shouted, "Mr. Chairman, I move that the UAW print Professor Lynd's speech in pamphlet form and have it made available to UAW locals." The motion was carried unanimously. At last we radicals had a piece of UAW literature that went to the root of things! I used the Lynd pamphlet with good effect in my classes, in short talks at union meetings, and in my *Voice of Local 212* column. I also used it when I was invited to talk before Wayne State University students. Needless to say, Professor Lynd was never again invited to address a UAW education conference.

Windmills

Looking back, I can see that we socialists in the UAW tilted at windmills too long. Al Nash said it well: "We've played the Labor Party theme for years, but we are farther away from a labor party than we ever were." He was right. Except for a handful of radicals, auto workers were firmly committed to the Democratic Party. Labor Party advocates made no more impression on the union membership than a June bug makes on an iron rail. Socialists were like a man trying to ride two horses going in different directions. As an education director, I was paid to teach UAW policy, and UAW policy was opposed to a labor party. A socialist should tell workers how the great corporations exercise a controlling influence over presidents, senators, congressmen, and governors, but the union teaches that American domestic and foreign problems can be resolved by the Democratic Party. No wonder that most socialists whom I knew decided to give up their ambivalent role. They ceased to be socialists and became good unionists, adhering strictly to the UAW line. Moreover, they became overly sensitive about their political past; they always seemed to be on the defensive when in the presence of acknowledged Socialists.

This was notably true of former Socialists in the UAW hierarchy (officials and heads of administrative departments). They went out of their way to insult radicals and denounce known Socialists in the union. Socialists were accorded more courtesy and respect by those UAW officials and administrators who had no Socialist background, but who were just good union guys. My guess is that the former Socialists somehow felt threatened by those of us who did not try to "live down" our Socialist convictions. In the presence of Socialists, they acted mighty uncomfortably. I remember the time at a UAW convention when Judah Drob (then the Detroit Socialist Party organizer) and I were talking with Norman Thomas in a hotel lobby. Leonard Woodcock walked by us and when Norman greeted him with a cheery "hello," Woodcock brusquely ignored him. I was shocked, for I knew that Woodcock once considered himself a disciple of Norman Thomas. When I told this to Norman, he nodded and smiled, as if to say, "I understand, and to understand is to forgive."

Why did these former comrades behave that way? Perhaps because their radical past made them feel insecure. This was true not only during the Joe McCarthy period, but long after McCarthy passed away. However, I believe it is no longer true today. Quite a number of former Socialists and Communists have been added to the UAW staff over the past dozen years. Why not? Most of them are competent people and take second place to no one in their loyalty to the UAW and its commitment to the Democratic Party. Moreover, these former radicals—former members of the SP, CP, and ISL—have not and cannot shed everything they learned in their radical youth, when they helped to generate the ideological ferment that later fed into the creation of the UAW and left its mark on this union as an institution. If the UAW continues to operate in the tradition of Reutherism, thanks will be due largely to the former radicals who occupy key posts in the UAW.

What a far cry the tradition of Reutherism is from the vision we radicals had in the early days, when we were so naive as to believe that the CIO crusade contained a revolutionary potential! Even some of the most brilliant minds on the left shared these illusions. In 1935, A.J. Muste wrote:

The question arises: if the general trend is as we have indicated, toward the broadening of the mass organizations, increase in their militancy, acceptance of Marxian leadership, struggle on a broader scale and a higher and higher political plane, etc., then is it not likely that the unions as a whole will, so far as the industrial sections of the country are concerned, become the workers' councils, the instruments of workers' power? Thus, the Central Labor Union—now, of course, with workers of all categories in its affiliated unions—becomes the Soviet of a given city; and the national union-federation convention, with its delegates from all industries and sections of the country, becomes the industrial part of the national congress of Soviets.

Was the American working class revolutionary in the 1930s? Or are those liberals (who were once radicals) correct when they argue that the American workers did not want a revolution; they simply wanted jobs, higher wages, and better working conditions? I can't presume to give a final answer one way or another to this question, but on the basis of what I experienced and observed in the 1930s, I offer the following tentative explanation.

I know for a fact that the workers did do revolutionary things and expressed revolutionary thoughts. Surely the United States government, from President Roosevelt's administration on down to state and local levels, realized the revolutionary mood of the workers and so did the labor leadership. In some areas working-class militancy was expressed by violence and murder; in other places it was derailed by massive New Deal concessions and collective bargaining gains. Roosevelt's administration and the labor bureaucracy combined to channel revolutionary tendencies in reformist directions. By revolutionary tendencies I mean the struggle to control their own life and work. I believe the labor leaders like John L. Lewis, Sidney Hillman, Phil Murray, and Walter Reuther were fully aware of this revolutionary mood and were determined to deflect it by bureaucratizing the CIO unions and institutionalizing grievance procedure to prevent direct action on the job.

In this they were ably helped by the leftist parties, especially the Communist Party. And even those of us who advocated the formation of a labor party—didn't we also help to deflect the revolutionary trends into reformist paths? For what is a labor party but a reformist party? When in power the British Labor Party ably administered British capitalism and did not hesitate to use armed force to break strikes when the occasion arose. What could a labor party in Michigan have done for the working people that the Democratic Party did not do when "Soapy" Williams was governor? Anyone who takes the trouble to read through the late Walter Reuther's speeches will soon discern that his perspective was that of a right-wing social democrat. And he believed that the kind of social democratic program he favored could best be achieved by working within the Democratic Party. Is it any wonder that Walter and the other top-ranking UAW officers, especially former Socialists like Leonard Woodcock and Emil Mazey, became so fiercely vindictive toward those radicals who exposed the Democratic Party as a party dedicated to perpetuating capitalism?

Union Democracy

Early in 1958 I began to explore the problem of union democracy. I wrote a series of articles on the subject in my *Voice of Local 212* column. The series began with a long review of S.M. Lipset's book describing the two-party system in the International Typographer's Union. I compared the electioneering process in that union with that in UAW locals. In the printers union, when two parties engage in an election campaign each party is permitted to state its case in the official union paper; each party is allowed equal time to present its program at the membership meeting; each side has access to the union's facilities for running off campaign literature. I pointed out that just the opposite of all this happens in UAW locals, where the incumbents are able to deny such democratic rights to their opponents. I also explained that the gap between the earnings of a printer and the salaries received by his union officers and representatives is not nearly as large as in the UAW. My review disturbed the officers of Local 212 and also some of the international UAW officials. Emil Mazey told me the review should never have appeared in the *Voice of Local 212*. And Art Vega, assistant to regional director Ken Morris, told me: "Ken got sore as hell when he read your review."

For some reason, a rash of books and magazine articles on union democracy appeared around that time. Some of the writers proposed sensible safeguards to guarantee elementary democratic rights for union members. I listed such proposed safeguards in my column and also submitted them for discussion in my Local 212 classes. The response was enthusiastic—so enthusiastic that some of the students proposed that the bylaws of Local 212 be amended to include some of the safeguards. "Our local can pioneer in becoming a truly democratic union local," they suggested. Three students volunteered to draw up a resolution on democratic safeguards and present it to a forthcoming membership meeting for consideration. But as it turned out I was not eligible to attend that meeting, for in April 1958 the officers of Local 212, on orders from their international regional director, fired me "for economy reasons." "Our local can no longer afford to pay a full-time education director," they said.

I Do Ad Hoc Assignments

Two weeks after I was fired from Local 212, I was hired to do ad hoc teaching assignments for Larry Rogin, director of the University of Michigan Labor and Industrial Relations Institute. I found the work very interesting, for it enabled me to learn about the kinds of problems workers were faced with in different industries—paper, steel, chemical, and others. Then in 1960 I began a new experience in workers' education when Larry put me in charge of setting up a program for an Italian labor team, which led to similar programs for other foreign labor teams. My duties consisted of bringing in resource people to lecture on American culture, American government, collective bargaining, labor arbitration, and so on. I taught an extended course on the history, philosophy, goals, and achievements of the American labor movement. What I enjoyed most about my duties were the field trips—taking the team to visit places like Solidarity House, union locals, factories, and management personnel offices. All five teams I worked with expressed a desire to meet Walter Reuther, so I always arranged a session in Solidarity House, where Louise Levinson and her aides briefed the team members about the UAW, its history, struggles, collective bargaining gains, fringe benefit innovations, administrative departments, education program, and so on. The foreign unionists were deeply impressed by what they learned at these sessions. And their brief meeting with Walter Reuther seemed to be the highlight of their four-month stay in the United States.

They were also deeply impressed, but in a different way, when they visited auto factories and UAW locals. For example, a tour through the Ford Rouge plant was followed by a meeting with officers of Ford Local 600, who explained their official duties and especially their labor contract difficulties with Ford management. I shall never forget the perceptive observation expressed by a member of our first Indonesian team after we visited the Plymouth plant and then talked with local union officers and a committeeman. The Indonesians were entranced by what they saw in the final assembly department, where operations were so intricately synchronized that every part came to the right place at the right time and every worker on the line performed his task with clockwork precision as the chassis moved along the conveyor.

A company tour guide accompanied us from department to department, sounding like a broken record as he made his canned spiel. I had asked the Plymouth UAW local to provide a committeeman to go with us on the factory tour. As the company guide intoned the virtues of Plymouth's coordinated production process, "all perfected to lighten the burden of labor and to produce the best car in the given price range," the committeeman muttered, "What a crock of crap that is! Wait till I tell you what it's really like." And when we went to the union local hall he told the Indonesians the facts of factory life. He cited example after example of speedup, health hazards, and management's refusal to settle legitimate grievances. He told about recent wildcat strikes over production standards and how the company charged the steward with provoking the wildcat and fired him. "We know damn well it was not the steward who provoked the wildcat; it was the line speed," the Indonesians were told. Then the committeeman showed us a dozen written grievances which had been pending for weeks. "Every day in the plant, guys come up to me and ask when to hell their grievances will get settled. Can you blame them if they lose patience and walk out?" the committeeman said.

As we left the union hall, the Indonesian unionist I referred to above turned to me and said, "You know, there are really two UAW's. There is the UAW we heard about in the Solidarity House—the UAW that wins pay raises, good pensions, more vacation pay, guaranteed wages, and things like that every time it bargains for a new contract. Then there is the UAW we hear about in union locals—the UAW that can't make General Motors, Chrysler, and Ford stop driving workers like machines." Later that day he asked me why Walter Reuther didn't get tougher with the employers about working conditions in the plants. I told him that many workers ask that same question.

The International

In 1963, I worked in the international UAW education department preparing materials and teaching classes at UAW locals and at summer schools. Sometimes I was also assigned to brief foreign labor teams when they visited Solidarity House. One time when Roy Reuther and I were picked to brief a German labor team, Roy told them about the UAW's political action policies, and I explained the international union's adminstrative setup. During the question period, one of the German unionists asked Roy why American labor did not have its own independent party but supported an acknowledged capitalist party. Roy explained why the UAW is more interested in political realignment than in advocating a labor party. He told about the various third party attempts in this country—how they arose, what they did in their brief span, and why they faded. To show how a major party can "steal the thunder" away from a third party, he quoted FDR's quip to Norman Thomas in 1934: "You know, Norman, we carried out 90 percent of your Socialist Party program."

The Germans listened intently, and when Roy concluded the team leader asked, "Ah, yes, but why don't you have a labor party?" Roy and I looked at each other; he grinned and asked, "Do you want to try?" I declined with thanks, for I had had the same experience time after time when dealing with foreign unionists, some of whom had lived in this country for several years. They simply could not comprehend the American political system. Parenthetically, this is also true of some of my closest radical friends who have lived in the United States for twenty years or more and who, in their youth, were active in European radical movements. They view American conditions through European spectacles and accordingly are baffled by "the American way of life."

Something else worth mentioning occurred when Roy and I talked with that German labor team. It was customary when teams visited the UAW to have them come to Solidarity House first and later visit a union local. To prepare the Germans for their meeting with local officers, I quoted from the international constitution and local bylaws so they could know how local unions are governed. One of the team members asked whether a local had the right to strike if it deemed strike action necessary. As always when answering such specific questions, I gave a concrete example drawn from actual experience. I explained that in terms of the formal constitutional framework workers have the right to strike over working conditions, but in actual practice it does not always work out that way. As I proceeded to elaborate on this, Roy cut me off abruptly: "You are getting off the subject; stick to telling them about UAW administrative structure!" Then he announced it was time to take a coffee break. After the break, we did not reassemble; the team was taken to Local 174 for further briefing.

Someone said that an institution, like an individual, always likes to put its best foot forward. Visitors who go to Solidarity House to learn about the UAW hear only the favorable side. Leaflets and pamphlets turned out by the education department are given the "UAW twist." Once when he told me to write up a leaflet, Bill MacDonald, then assistant education director, said, "Write it in terms of our prejudices." When I asked, "Is this an education department or a propaganda mill?," he grinned knowingly. Bill was a Canadian Socialist, and he and I always got along well. We were very candid with each other, and I felt free to say what was on my mind. Once when I told him that people who work for the Wayne State University Labor Relations Institute have more freedom to teach than people who work for the UAW, he agreed: "What to hell do you expect? The union has a political line. Our education department grinds out the kind of propaganda that indoctrinates our members to accept that line, just as our research department doctors statistics to support the UAW's economic claims. Be realistic . . . if it's objectivity you want, then get a job in some academic ivory tower!"

If Bill were still alive and teaching at Black Lake, would he argue the same way? Or would he find that UAW education has taken on a new dimension? An attractive booklet about Black Lake tells us ". . . members and their families participate in a rare kind of learning program. Emphasis is on shared experience . . . discussions, workshops, mock union conventions. Workshop programs range from collective bargaining to social problems."

The same kind of summer school "core" programs are being conducted at Black Lake as were conducted in the Lakeport summer schools I attended. Thus a brochure tells us: "The week-long schools will conduct mock bargaining sessions between 'union' and 'management' committees based on UAW's bargaining program and will examine the economics of bargaining and the connection between bargaining and the ballot box." By "ballot box" they mean pro-Democratic Party politics.

"Ghosts Within"

When I worked in Solidarity House, I often ate lunch in the union cafeteria and talked with UAW representatives who happened to be seated at the same table. Some of them were old friends who once attended classes I conducted in their union local. Frequently we talked nostalgically about "the good old days," and they related incidents from their early organizing experience. One day I had a long discussion with Pat Quinn, who was then an international representative in the UAW political action department. Pat was in poor health, and he told me he was "countin' the days till I can retire." Although he was earning a good salary and could look forward to a substantial pension upon retirement, he was not happy in Solidarity House. "Look around here," he said, with a sweep of his arm. "What do you see? Many of these international reps are broken down old union war horses like me."

Then, mixing metaphors, he continued, "We're ghosts, that's what we are, the ghosts within. When my opposition in Dodge Local 3 defeated me the last time I ran for president, Walter Reuther called me to his office . . . you know, I belonged to the anti-Reuther slate. Walter offered me a job in the International; he knew damn well that if I went back in the shop, I'd stir things up . . . I'd build a strong group and unseat the pro-Reuther administration in the next local election. That's the last thing Walter wanted, so he put me on the international payroll to get me to hell out of Dodge local. Walter's a sharp operator; he knows how to weaken his opposition in UAW locals. You'd be surprised at all the reps on the staff who were one-time political enemies; even some who were known Communists. I'll be frank; we got bought off. Some of my union local caucus friends accused me of selling out. In a way, I did. But what kind of a fool would I be if I didn't accept Walter's offer? At my age and with my broken health, how long would I last if I went back to the Dodge paint shop? I've been out of the factory for years; if I had to go back now and buck production, I'd probably drop dead in a week's time!"

I reminded Pat Quinn that many UAW international staff people were qualified technicians: time-study engineers, insurance actuaries, professional news writers, research statisticians, lawyers, and so on. Pat admitted that such specialists are needed: "I never finished grade school and guys like me can't even interpret the Chrysler contract without the help of experts, but let me tell you something . . . that's just what's wrong with this union. It's run more and more by experts!" Then he cited an example to show what he meant:

You remember Lloyd Jones . . . he was a hillbilly preacher from the south, and when he came to Detroit in the early thirties he got a job in an auto plant and soon helped to organize the workers in his department. He was a fiery orator, only instead of preaching against hellfire, he now fumed against "the industrial pharaohs who grind down their factory slaves."

Jones was elected and re-elected president of UAW Murray Body Local 2. And after the Murray Body plant went bankrupt, Jones was put on the UAW international staff. He didn't stay long, and he told me why he quit. He said that the job made him feel like a useless hack. Day after day, he sat in his office with nothing to do. Then one time they sent him to help organize a parts plant on the East Side of Detroit. Jones was a damn good organizer and had a lot of experience. He called together the active union people who worked in the plant and asked them to list all the grievances that workers were complaining about. Then Jones composed a leaflet around those gut issues and asked his UAW superior to have copies mimeographed so they could be passed out to workers on the morning shift. Jones's boss bawled him out. He said the International already had a large supply of organizing literature and no other kind was to be passed out. Jones read the International leaflet and protested that it sounded like something written by a professor; he said workers won't even read such stuff but after the first sentence would toss it on the street. He was told not to question orders, but to carry them out. He did . . . and later phoned his boss in Solidarity House and suggested he come to the plant and see how the workers threw the UAW leaflets on the street.

Another UAW international staff member who told me how the "outside experts" are taking over more and more functions of the union was Robert Kanter. Bob, now a University of Connecticut professor, had been an international representative for over thirty years and during that long time served variously as field organizer, time-study engineer, social security analyst, and specialist in the auditing department. He told me that more and more "outside experts," who had no previous shop and union experience, were being brought into Solidarity House: "How can those people be expected to have empathy with auto workers? This is not the least of the reasons why the international union is becoming ever more estranged from the membership."

No Solidarity

But Kanter at least knew that the membership was becoming increasingly alienated from the international union. The top-ranking officers and their close adminstrative assistants do not seem to be aware of this phenomenon. A case in point occurred about five years ago when I attended a rally of Michigan migrant workers; the rally was called to protest the substandard wages and miserable working conditions of migrant labor, mostly Mexican, employed by Michigan farmers. Although the rally had been advertised in the daily press and announcements had been sent to UAW locals, not more than four UAW members bothered to show up. Considerably more members from other unions, especially Myra Wolfgang's Hotel, Restaurant and Bartender's Union, turned out to lend moral support to the migrants.

The labor reporter for the *Detroit Free Press* interviewed people at the rally for comments. When he came to me, I told him that UAW members no longer respond, as they once did, when their leaders call on them to help less fortunate workers who struggle to get above the poverty line. A few days later I received a letter from Irving Bluestone, then chief administrative assistant to Walter Reuther and now a UAW vice president. He took issue with what I told the reporter. He reminded me that the UAW has always been generous in giving financial and other help to struggling unions when they were in need. He also reminded me that the UAW has a good record of fighting for social justice on economic, social, and political levels, and he listed specific examples.

However, Bluestone and I were talking about different things! He was talking about the international UAW, the officers, and the executive board—the hierarchy that controls the policy-making machinery of the UAW. I was talking about the membership, the rank and file. After the hierarchy's reducing the union to a one-party state, after separating themselves from the membership, after consistently stamping out any signs of militancy in the rank and file—then its financial contributions and sweeping statements of support are no reasons for rank and file workers to rally to the hierarchy's cause, any more than workers get excited by contributions and activity for the Democratic Party and the social causes designed to take people's minds off the problems *inside* the factories. If workers don't rally to the UAW call to support farm workers, it is, perhaps, because they are not faucets to be turned on and off at will by their leadership. I see no reason to assume, given a means to express their own views and a leadership that is *relevant*, that workers would not express their class loyalty. A union which can recruit 700 union officials to help break a wildcat strike at the Detroit Mack Avenue plant (as happened recently) can't complain when workers don't respond to "legitimate" calls to action.

When the official leadership is no longer relevant to the workers in the shops, then the more militant workers begin to form caucuses, and such caucuses are now springing up in the UAW. They make themselves heard, and they are anathema to UAW International officers and representatives and quite often to the officers in their own union locals. They band together in groups, such as the United Rank and File Caucus, which has members in different states and recently held a national conference where they formulated their program in resolutions demanding that the UAW make a determined fight for humanized working conditions, an end to compulsory overtime, revamped grievance procedure, a thirty-two hour work week, a steward for every foreman, and so on. In every issue of its publication the United Caucus calls upon organized labor in general, and the UAW in particular, to sever connections with the Democratic Party and "build a labor party." UAW international representatives were incensed when the United Caucus published figures which exposed the widening gap between the bureaucracy and the membership as reflected in the differences in income. "In recent years, staff salaries have risen faster than wages earned by auto workers, and staff benefits have reached levels much closer to those of minor corporation executives than to those of auto workers," the United Caucus reported.

Concerned Unionists

The moving spirits in these rank and file groups are radicals, usually former Communists or Trotskyites, who prefer to work in the plant and remain close to the rank and file rather than become "union porkchoppers." An outstanding example is Irving Canter, who organized the Concerned Unionists, a small group in Detroit consisting mostly of skilled tradesmen like himself. Wherever there is labor trouble, the Concerned Unionists are on the scene, their placards proclaiming solidarity with the embattled workers. They march in picket lines, participate in grape and lettuce boycotts on behalf of the United Farm Workers, and pass out their program demands at UAW conferences and conventions.

In his youth Canter attended the University of Texas, where he first became active in the Trotsky movement. During the depression he worked on WPA, translating medical papers into French and Spanish. He told me that his first factory job was on the assembly line, and he decided that any radical who wants to work in the shop should learn a trade. He observed that young radicals who take factory jobs so they "can be with workers" soon quit because they simply cannot stand the terrible monotony and speedup. This is why Canter became a toolmaker. In his local union he attended every meeting and always "called the shots as he saw them." To many of the white workers he was a "nigger lover" because he did not hesitate to criticize the UAW for allowing management to practice discrimination when hiring apprentices: "There should be more blacks admitted to the skilled trades." When the international UAW officers, including Walter Reuther and Leonard Woodcock (but not Emil Mazey), endorsed President Lyndon Johnson's Vietnam war policy, Canter denounced that policy and argued at every union meeting that the UAW should launch a crash education campaign to let auto workers know the truth about the American government's reactionary genocidal war in Vietnam: "Why is the international leadership afraid to speak out against the war? Is it because the union is an appendage to the Democratic Party and we dare not embarrass Johnson's administration? Do we have to wait until a Republican president occupies the White House before the UAW takes a strong stand against the horror we are unleashing in Vietnam?"

The Concerned Unionists regularly issue a four-page mimeographed bulletin, which they distribute at factory gates. Their bulletin reminds me of the shop papers put out by the CP in the 1920s and early 1930s. Each issue focuses on concrete problems that deeply concern workers in the shops, such as compulsory overtime. And each issue calls for returning democracy to the membership: "This union was once controlled from the bottom up by the workers who organized it; today it is controlled from the top down by a bureaucracy, by a tightly knit political machine which centers in Solidarity House and reaches into every UAW region and union local. Control has been alienated, separated, divorced from the rank and file."

How to achieve democratic control of the union? I discussed this question many times when conducting classes in UAW halls. This theme invariably brought up another subject: "How can we persuade workers to attend meetings?" All sorts of gimmicks were suggested: give door prizes, show an interesting film at the beginning of meetings, serve refreshments at the close of meetings, and so on. In the early days the workers knew that meetings were relevant to them; they decided policies that had a direct bearing on their working lives. Today union meetings are basically irrelevant, and the workers are aware of this fact. Here is how a Local 212 member said it:

Is it any wonder that barely enough workers show up at a meeting to make a quorum? And why should they attend meetings? Most of those who attend are union politicians and their supporters who belong to competing factions. Those on one side show up at meetings to make sure that those on the other side don't pull something over on them. Workers in the shop know it doesn't make any difference to them which faction gets elected. You sit through meetings and listen to long spiels about things that don't mean a damn to us guys in the shop. The officers sound off about how important it is to support Democratic Party candidates and donate money to COPE (Committee on Political Education). Hell, the workers couldn't care less about COPE. But they do care about conditions in the shop—about speedup and pollution and health and safety hazards and things like that. And they know only too well that when such problems are raised at union meetings nothing happens. The officers tell us that such problems are grievances and we should refer them to the grievance machinery and not bring them up at union meetings. And so we have to waste our time in those meetings listening to a lot of boring talk about things that don't mean a damn to us one way or another. Can you blame us for not attending meetings?

Humanizing Working Conditions

The erosion of union democracy is directly linked to the problem of "humanizing working conditions." Ever since the General Motors assembly plant in Norwood, Ohio, was shut down for six months over the issue of speedup, leading newspapers and magazines including the *Wall Street Journal, New York Times, Harpers,* and the *New York Review*, have carried detailed stories about how young workers rebel against the speed and monotony of automated production. Thus *Harpers* in August 1972 printed an exchange of letters between Irving Bluestone and Barbara Carson concerning "Boredom on the Assembly Line." In a letter to *Harpers* I commented on the exchange: "With the best will in the world, I cannot agree with Mr. Bluestone (whom I know personally and whom I regard as an exceedingly knowledgeable union administrator) when he says that 'improvement of working conditions has been given as high priority by the union as have wages and benefits.' To the contrary, I believe that a well-documented case can be made to the effect that over the years, contractual relations between the union and the corporations have become institutionalized in such a way that the UAW has been trading off working conditions for economic gains. And I seriously question that working conditions can be humanized within the present framework of institutionalized collective bargaining."

Shortly after writing that letter I learned that Leonard Woodcock acknowledged that the Norwood workers, after a 174-day strike, and also the Lordstown workers, who struck for 23 days earlier in 1972, ended up where they began on the speedup dispute. Auto workers have battled speedup for more than forty years, and today General Motors is the worst offender. To win this battle, Woodcock and the UAW leadership would have to mobilize the workers for an all-out fight to compel General Motors to humanize its production process. This the UAW hierarchy will never do.

A few years ago I had a long talk with a young auto worker who couldn't understand why the UAW, when it bargains with management, places more emphasis on fringe benefits like pensions than on working conditions: "The way I have to work my ass off on the Plymouth assembly line, hell, I'll be dead long before my pension time arrives!" I told him what it was like to work in auto plants when I was his age; how the companies took advantage of unemployment to cut wages to depression levels; how workers had to buy the foreman whiskey or paint his garage in order to keep their jobs; how some workers used shoe polish to conceal their gray hairs when applying for a job because in those pre-union days employment agents were guided by the rule "too old at forty"; how straw bosses behaved not like human beings but like brutal slave drivers toward the men under them; how workers frequently reported for work in the morning only to be told by the foreman, "there's no stock, so stick around until some shows up," but when no stock arrived by noon, the men were sent home and received no pay for that day; how the companies installed a bonus system no one could ever figure out, so that very often the harder men worked, the less money they earned; how auto companies operated their equipment at a feverish pace to produce the new models and then abruptly laid off people in droves (and in those days there was no such thing as unemployment compensation and no unemployment supplemental benefits such as union contracts now provide); how foremen in the Dodge plant used to invite second-shift women to accompany them to the roof at night and made life miserable for those who refused the invitation; how the Briggs press steel department was called "the butcher shop" because of the high accident rate due to speedup and lax safety measures; how blacks were confined to cleaning toilets or performing the dirtiest, hottest tasks in foundries, with no chance for promotion to better jobs; how women were paid substantially less than men for doing comparable jobs.

Then I told my young friend that by January 1933 the auto workers couldn't take it any more and all hell broke loose when a rash of strikes erupted in Michigan and countinued to erupt month after month until they culminated in the General Motors sit-down strike. "If the auto workers back in that period could compel the mightiest industrial corporation in the world to surrender at the bargaining table, then surely your generation can find a way to exercise more control over production so that factory work will no longer be a daily hell," I told him.

His response was quick: "You old guys always brag about your early victories. No one in his right mind will deny that they were great victories. Fringe benefits are fine; paid vacations, pensions, holiday pay—all are fine. But how about what goes on in the shop? You old birds should work in the shop on some of those unsafe machines, slip on those oily floors, stumble over castings and stock boxes that clutter the aisles, breathe in the fumes and chemicals, work your ass off to keep up on the line, shiver in winter when there's not enough heat, and swelter in summer when there's no ventilation."

I told him he described working conditions much as they were when I worked in the plants back in the twenties.

"Then what in hell happened to your boasted victories? I don't mean fringes, but working conditions. Why did your victories on the shop floor turn into defeats?" I told him why I thought the victories were turned into their opposite. In the early days workers could settle grievances on the job. Then the stewards had power—power to call workers off the job until those grievances were settled. But later a thing called labor-management relations took power away from stewards. A no-strike pledge was added to the contracts, which gave management the right to fire workers and stewards involved in work stoppages. That no-strike pledge turned the union into a disciplinary agent. Here is a sample clause: "During the life of this agreement the union will not cause or permit its members to cause, nor will any member of the union take part in sit-down, stay-in, or slowdown in any plant of the company."

I told him that later something else was added—a so-called management sole prerogative clause, which reads something like the following: "The right to hire, promote, discharge, or discipline for cause; and to maintain discipline and efficiency of employees, is the sole responsibility of the corporation except that union members shall not be discriminated against as such. In addition, the products to be manufactured, the methods, processes, and means of manufacturing are solely the responsibility of the corporation."

A third factor—probably the most decisive one—is the fact that following Walter Reuther's complete victory in 1947, the UAW's democratic kind of factionalism was rapidly transformed into a one-party state, and the Reuther administration worked hand-in-hand with management to discipline workers. In the early days we could truly say the union was controlled by and run for the workers. This has long since ceased to be true. Today there is a union-management framework that has the workers boxed in. The union constitution is stacked against them, so is the union contract, so are the well-heeled International officers and representatives. And if the workers rebel against this formidable combination they will soon learn that government boards, the courts, and the forces of law and order are stacked against them.

Workers Talk

Clearly the new, younger, better-educated generation of workers will learn through bitter experience that they cannot achieve decent working conditions through the rigidly institutionalized union structure. They must forge altogether new organs of struggle. What forms these struggles will take no one can say in advance. In this connection I shall never forget the very last class I conducted in steward training. I began the last session of that six-lesson course by asking the students (all were stewards) what kind of grievances the workers complained about in the shop. I listed the grievances one by one on the blackboard. Then I conducted a discussion on each grievance in all its implications. When an instructor limits discussion to the formal aspects of grievance procedure, his session invariably becomes dull and boring. But when he encourages discussion on day-to-day working conditions, the students come up with vivid, graphic accounts of factory life. On that day I heard comments like the following:

"Yesterday I cut my finger on the sharp edge of a flange. When I went to the so-called factory hospital, they talked to me like I was a dog."

"The other day when I came back from the toilet the foreman bawled me out for taking too long. He said he trained himself to go to the toilet right after breakfast at home and told me I could train myself the same way."

"They expect you to get out the same amount of work every hour in the day, even if you have to work four hours overtime. Hell, a man ain't a machine."

"When you work on the motor line, the motors keep coming at you all the time. If you take time to blow your nose the motor moves past you and you have to rush to do your operation in time to catch the next motor as it comes by."

"Last week a guy in my department complained about a sore back and said he couldn't keep up with his workload. What did the foreman do? He transferred the guy to the pit. That's where you stand up in a gutter under the chassis and you have to reach up and do your operation as the chassis moves along the line over you. The guys call it Siberia."

"When work starts on a new model—that's when operations are speeded up. So you file a grievance with the steward, the steward refers it to the foreman. Then the steward and the foreman work out a verbal adjustment which makes it easier for the workers. Then about two or three days later—bingo!—the speed gets right back to where it was."

"You hear a lot about city pollution these days. It's nothing compared to the pollution where I work: fumes, dirt, lead. We complain to the steward, the steward complains to the plant committee, the plant committee raises hell with supervision. Supervision makes promises, but promises don't remove the pollution."

Somewhere the late Harvey Swados wrote that an industrial worker may insist that he belongs to the middle class, he may drive a middle-class automobile, live in a middle-class suburb, "own" a middle-class home, mingle in a middle-class community, but by God when he takes his place in the factory he lives like a worker! There is nothing middle-class about the totality of the factory milieu.

In my steward classes I have often drawn a large circle on the blackboard and listed in the circle all the different types of grievances mentioned by the students. Then I asked if they could think of any other grievance which no one had mentioned so far. One time a young woman from the West Side Local 174 spoke up:

"Yes, I can think of another grievance that is not listed in your circle—boredom!" At first the other students laughed. Then I asked: "Is boredom a grievance in terms of the contract?" My question touched off a heated discussion that lasted an hour. How I wish I had taped that discussion! It soon centered around one question: Can boredom be eliminated from factory production work? One worker in an angry voice demanded: "How in hell can boredom be taken out of the assembly line?" Another student replied: "Maybe boredom can't be eliminated completely, but the union can at least see to it that work becomes less boring."

At that point I broke the class into buzz sessions, into three groups (there were about twenty-five students), and asked them to meet in different sections of the hall and come up with ideas about how to deal with the problem of boredom. Fifteen minutes later I called them together, outlined their ideas on the blackboard, and then called for general discussion. At first most of the students insisted that the union could not cope with the problem of boredom, except by reducing the total work time, that is, by contract clauses providing for longer paid vacations, more paid holidays, and earlier retirement. Some members in the class argued that boredom could be eliminated or greatly reduced if the work process were rearranged. I summarized the thinking of those people as follows:

"As long as a worker is forced to toil on the same operation day after day, week after week, year after year, he is sure to find his job boring. But how about reorganizing work? Why should a worker be stuck on the same job permanently? Why not, say, work on a drill press two hours, then on a milling machine two hours, then on the assembly line, then on the bench? Then the next day be switched to other jobs. And why does a production worker always have to remain a production worker? Why can't he be upgraded to skilled work, trained to do skilled work? Yes, give people an opportunity to learn all kinds of skills, even to engineering or chemistry or other technical jobs? And let engineers and technicians and office workers do their stint on the assembly line."

For the sake of exploring ideas I asked the class to imagine what could be done if the work process were extended to include the entire community and not just the factory: "Imagine the people in the entire community planning how work is to be performed. During the year a person could spend a portion of his work time hauling garbage, another portion delivering milk, another portion teaching school, another portion doing factory work, and so on. At one time a worker would be a teacher, at another time a machinist, at another time a carpenter, then something else. Work and education would go hand-in-hand, and education would be a life-long process. Opportunities for all-around individual development would be infinitely greater than is the case today."

Workers' Councils

Someone in the class said that such a system might exist in heaven but never in the real world, and then he asked: "Where has the sort of thing you describe ever taken place in this or any other country?" I answered by telling the class about the workers' councils that sprang up in Hungary during the Hungarian Revolution in 1956—how hundreds of councils arose in a spontaneous movement across the country; how the central demand of those councils called for workers' management of production; how in the provinces the workers had taken over a number of radio stations and used them to beam the truth about the aims of the workers' councils, such as political and civil liberty, for independent trade unions and freedom for all political parties, for the complete withdrawal of Russian troops, for an end to the kind of elections in which the Communist Party imposed a single list of candidates, for the complete right of the people to choose their own representatives.

I explained how the councils began to link up. In the cities the councils consisted of delegates of councils in the area. Some of these councils included representatives from white-collar workers, from farmers in the area, from the army, and from the professions. I reminded the students that the GM sit-down was conducted by a network of committees and that in the Seattle general strike of 1919 a network of committees actually determined the productive affairs of the city while the strike lasted. I said that what was shaping up in Hungary was a vast web of councils through which the working people, blue-collar and white-collar, would democratically manage the production and distribution of goods and services. But this did not happen because the workers' council movement was crushed by Russian tanks.

"Do you think anything like that could ever happen here?" a student asked. I related what a Flint sit-downer told me in January 1973: "When we took over the plants we set up a government, a government of committees; all our activities were planned by committees. If we had to, we could have operated the plants by committees and made a better job of it than management does. Who gets out production when the plants operate? Who machines the parts and assembles the cars and works on the lines? The workers do all that. And if they can do it to make stockholders rich why can't they do it for themselves—I mean why can't the working people run the factories and the mines and the farms and the offices for the benefit of all the people?"

Usually when a class period ends, the students lose no time heading for their cars in the parking lot. This time they gathered in little groups and carried on the discussion loud and long. We began with a discussion of the work process and what could be done under the labor contract and then explored the possibilities far beyond the limits of the contract. I wonder what would happen if an instructor attempted to conduct such a session at Black Lake today?

My only purpose in opening up that long discussion of workers' councils was to let the students know that "workers' control" is no mere abstract concept but a form of organization that sprang up in the Paris Commune of 1871, in the early days of the Russian Revolution, and again for a brief period during the Hungarian Revolution. I also told them where they could obtain pamphlets on the subject of workers' control.

Thought Control

And now I would like to sum up my view of workers' education. I have already indicated my belief that education as conducted by the UAW consists essentially of vocational training and indoctrination. By vocational training I mean such subjects as steward training, parliamentary law, public speaking, union administration, collective bargaining, and time study. These tool courses are absolutely necessary if key union members—stewards, committeemen, local officers, and international representatives—are to perform their duties competently. On this score there can be no disagreement. Not so with respect to indoctrination. When I taught at UAW summer schools (after 1947), what passed for "political education" was blatant indoctrination. Students were filled with propaganda to convince them that labor's best interests could be served by the Democratic Party. An instructor was not allowed to present the facts about the Democratic Party—for example, the facts about how that Party serves the interests of big business. I could give other examples of how an instructor was

One of the many groups that toured the UAW Black Lake Education Center in the spring of 1970. In the background is one of the covered walkways connecting the center's main buildings.

not permitted to present the pertinent facts. How can men and women in the labor movement be given sound workers' education without the relevant facts? In steward training classes the instructor stressed repeatedly that stewards must get "all the facts" before proceeding to negotiate with the foreman or the labor relations person. But such respect for facts is missing in political action classes.

World Workers Education Movements, written by Marius Hansome and published in 1931, is a historical and critical view of workers' education as it was conducted more than forty years ago in trade unions, cooperatives, and labor parties not only in America and Europe, but in countries as far away as Japan, India, and Australia. Though outdated in many ways, it is surprisingly timely in one important particular: the way in which workers' education is stifled by official unions. Consider the following extraordinary statement by John Kerchen, then director of workers' education at the University of California:

There are some things we teach in the University of California we wouldn't dare teach in the labor classes. We have classes in the study of social reform. That wouldn't be tolerated in the A.F. of L. Why, in the university we have a class in the history and theory of revolutions. Imagine my teaching that in the trade union classes! If we tried to we would get into trouble with the A.F. of L. We give the classes that the A.F.L. desires. There is no demand for classes in Marxism, radical economics, or questions on the control of industry. The A.F.L. accepts the present order of society. We are living in bad air, but we have to breathe it. We are not trying to change the air.

The UAW exercises such rigorous thought control over classes taught in its summer schools. I had much more freedom to teach when conducting classes sponsored by the Wayne State University Labor Relations Institute. So-called UAW education is aimed at sealing the mind against views other than those approved by the hierarchy. From personal experience I can report that the Wayne State University Labor Relations Institute encourages the kind of education that opens the mind and helps it to formulate its own conclusions. Here you have the difference between indoctrination and education.

Would an instructor at a UAW summer school dare teach the truth about the UAW itself? About the division between the union and the rank and file? About the way in which the membership is manipulated by the ruling apparatus? About how the spectacular victories won by the auto workers in the early days have been transmuted into their opposite by the institutionalized process of labor relations?

"Labor relations? That has nothing to do with us workers. Labor relations is something that goes on between the union representatives and company representatives," said an auto worker in one of my steward classes. His observation was more profound than he realized.

The UAW is widely hailed for its "social unionism"—for being a broad social movement concerned with securing justice for everyone. No other industrial union in America, we are told, is so concerned with civil rights, peace, foreign affairs, consumer protection, education, and economic policy. But, as I said before, there are two UAWs; one is noted for its social unionism. And the other one? This is the UAW that cooperates with management in disciplining workers on the job. At one of the last UAW summer school sessions that I conducted in steward training, I quoted the following passage from an article by Gene Richard that appeared in the *Atlantic Monthly* in April 1937:

There is a shrill note. It is impersonal, commanding, and it expresses the entire power which orders the wheels set in motion. The conveyor begins to move immediately. Mysteriously the men are in their places and at work. A man near me grasps the two handles of a wrench he holds all day long. This is the extent of his operation . . . one position, one job, all day.

Men about me are constantly cursing and talking filth. Something about the monotonous routine breaks down all restraint. The men in some cases have little in common, but they must talk. The work will not absorb the mind of the normal man, so they must think. Thus, without a trace of conscience, one speaks of his more intimate relations with his wife. We work on and on with spurts of conversation. Suddenly a man breaks forth with a mighty howl. Others follow. We set up a howling all over the shop. It is a relief, this howling.

Finally we are walking out, punching our cards. Laughter is now sincere, but weary. It is still dark on the outside. I am so dulled that I have gotten here without realizing it. I stop, ponder. I can't think where I parked my car; the morning was so long ago.

I asked the class: "Is factory life much different today from the way Richard described it?" I can still remember some of the replies: "That's just how it is in the shop! That's what it's like on the conveyor line! And that's exactly how the guys act and talk."

Irving Bluestone in his 1972 paper, "Democratizing the Work Place," quotes an auto assembly worker:

The feeling with me was that every working moment my whole life revolved around that lousy job. I'd get up in the morning at 4:30, eat and get myself together, drive to work. Work started at 6:30. I'd get home at 3:30 or 3:45, read a newspaper and go to bed. It seemed that every waking minute was involved in that job. On Saturdays and Sundays you'd spend the whole weekend dreading Mondays.

Is it any wonder that more and more factory workers are refusing to accept factory discipline as a law of nature? And as time goes on more and more workers will refuse to submit to the kind of factory discipline imposed on them by union and management under the terms of the union contract and the whole process of what is termed "labor relations."

The history of the AFL proves that when the organizational structure of the union movement becomes a fetter to the best interests of the workers, they break through the structure and develop new organs of struggle. The next big breakthrough in labor history will revolve around a new question: Who controls the work?

10 One-Party Unionism of the 1970s

In the introduction to *Rank and File—Personal Stories of Working Class Organizers*, Alice and Staughton Lynd wrote:

Once unions gained recognition and union dues were taken out of the workers' pay checks, unions took on a new character. The militancy, democracy and local union autonomy which flourished in the organizing period faded away or were crushed. Taking leadership in the union, which meant working for nothing and living with the risk of being beaten or killed, became a way of moving ahead personally. It was a way of getting out of the work place and getting a higher income. A successful local union officer could then go on to a career on the staff of the international union.

I have already explained how the once democratic UAW locals were gradually stripped of autonomy and changed into appendages of the international union. To indicate how the International evolved into a one-party state, I draw on five sources: (1) *Governing the UAW* by Jack Stieber; (2) *Labor Radical—A Personal History* by Len De Caux; (3) *The Company and the Union* by William Serrin; (4) testimony of union representatives; and (5) my own experiences and observations.

Stieber on the UAW

In his preface Stieber explains the purpose of his book: "This book deals only with the national government of the UAW. It does not concern itself with operations of the union at the regional or local level, except insofar as they directly affect the national government."

The book describes the formal structure and operations of the international UAW—how conventions are conducted, how national and regional caucuses are controlled from the top, how the elections of top officers and regional directors are manipulated, how the various departments function, and so on. Nowhere do we get the *feel* of how the bureaucracy exerts its power at the local level.

After briefly sketching the history of the UAW from its first convention in 1935 to the ascendancy of Walter Reuther und his supporters at the 1947 convention, Stieber describes the operation of the international union and, in the course of doing so, he reveals many of the procedures by which it became increasingly bureaucratized. A summary of these procedures follows.

Convention Committees

These committees play a very important role in connection with such vital matters as constitutional amendments, resolutions, credentials, grievances, and the like.

There was a time when committee reports could electrify a convention. But that happened in the days when the composition of committees reflected different factions. In those days committees submitted majority reports and minority reports and sometimes even "super-duper" minority reports. Delegates bristled with challenge as they debated heatedly for the report favoring their faction, and they castigated opposing reports. I can still remember the stormy debates touched off by majority and minority reports when the resolution on incentive pay was submitted to the delegates for consideration. The Communist Party members and their supporters vehemently supported incentive pay while their opponents, led by the Reuther brothers, just as vehemently denounced the incentive proposal.

But such opposing convention views are not fought out on the convention floor any more. Convention committee appointments are made by the international executive board from delegates recommended by board members. In the days when the executive board was split by factions, opposition delegates were appointed on committees. However, once the Reuther forces consolidated their hold over the executive board in 1949, opposition delegates were seldom appointed to committee posts, according to Stieber. And if any opposition member was appointed to a committee he soon became a "loyal oppositionist."

Workers who attend "union administration" courses at UAW summer schools are taught that the UAW is a democratic union because the membership elects delegates to the UAW convention and those delegates in turn formulate union policies. Nothing could be further from the truth. The most important policies adopted by the convention are formulated by committees, and those committees are not elected by the delegates. Actually committees start their work several days before the convention convenes. As Stieber writes: "In view of the important role occupied by the committees in union conventions—especially committees dealing with constitutional amendments, resolutions, credentials and grievances—the procedure followed by the UAW . . . makes it extremely difficult for the delegates to control the convention."

In union local meetings, members have the right to amend any proposal submitted for their consideration. UAW convention delegates do not have the right to amend committee reports. "Committee reports are not subject to amendment or substitution until they are voted down and resubmitted," writes Stieber. So not only do the delegates have no voice in the selection of committee members, they also have no right to amend reports which are read to them by hand-picked committees.

The ban on amendments or substitutions from the floor until a committee recommendation has been voted down, together with the absence of any voice by the convention in the selection of committee members, "tends to make the delegates' function one of approving or disapproving administration policies, rather than determining policy (which is the role in which the delegates see themselves)," says Stieber.

The almost complete absence of minority committee reports in recent conventions indicates that opposition elements within the union are not represented on committees. Committee reports are cut and dried, and convention resolutions are not drawn up by the resolution committee but written by technicians and publicity department experts. When these long-winded reports—some of them run over 1,500 words—are read by the committee chairman, the delegates read newspapers, carry on conversations, or daydream—and then vote routinely in favor of resolutions they have not read or even heard as they were being read.

The Fading Opposition
Stieber refers to delegates who complain that the chairman discriminates against opposition delegates. Often when seated in the visitors' gallery I observed how the chairman performed. He allowed committee members and officers to speak more often and for much longer periods than he granted opposition speakers. And when recognizing delegates from the floor, he conveniently overlooked known oppositionists, especially if they happened to be capable floor leaders.

Another device that helps the hierarchy to tighten its control over a convention is the rule which requires 30 percent of all delegates expected to attend a convention to force a roll call vote. Everyone knows that 30 percent of all delegates are never present at any one time; accordingly the roll call requirement is always higher than 30 percent, especially during the last sessions of the convention. "To make the requirement so prohibitive as to rule out roll call votes, for all practical purposes, makes mockery of the provision that delegates shall carry varying voting strength depending on the number of members they represent," observes Stieber.

Another rule which redounds to the advantage of incumbent officers forbids acceptance speeches by members nominated for international offices. This means that a man running for a top office has no right to explain his program from the convention platform.

Caucuses

In the days when the UAW was a truly democratic union, caucuses played a vital role in UAW politics. Speaking at the 1946 UAW convention, CIO President Philip Murray said:

Sometimes I have . . . wondered when you went over your constitution that you have not made provisions for time and a half for attending caucuses . . . because you surely work overtime. . . . There is no question about an automobile worker: when he finishes his day's work in the convention he is looking for a caucus at night. He doesn't care where the caucus is or who is holding it, he wants to go to a caucus.

In those days there was a two-way flow between the top officers and the rank and file. But that flow soon stopped after 1947. Only two years later, at the 1949 convention, a proposal to divide one region into two regions was being debated. Here is how one of the delegates saw the problem:

We talked of democracy and American unionism in this hall for three days and what do they try to do? The international executive board acts as a dictatorial power to cram something down our throats that you don't want and never heard of before this convention.
The general tendency in our union over the past years is to take the matters in this union out of the ranks and to let these policies be determined by smaller and smaller numbers of people; to the extent that we fail to mobilize the ranks of the union in the direct affairs of the union—to this extent will this union fail in its objective.

The days of the old fighting opposition caucuses have long since faded into oblivion. National and regional caucuses, which are called on the eve of the conventions, are controlled from the top; their function is merely to endorse recommendations made by the caucus steering committee, a 200-member body selected by the administration, Stieber writes. The regional caucus is useful to the regional director in much the same way as the national caucus serves the international officers: it helps him to gauge and manipulate rank and file sentiment.

The Past is Dead

Four years after gaining control of the UAW executive board, Walter Reuther boasted: "We are never going back to those old factional days; we are going ahead, and we are all going ahead together . . . the past is dead, as far as factional considerations are concerned."

UAW events moved swiftly toward a one-party state after Reuther's triumph in 1947. Strong opposition leaders like R.J. Thomas, Dick Frankensteen, and Dick Leonard left the UAW for employment elsewhere. Others were eliminated during elections. Staff members either accommodated the new oligarchy or were dismissed. I observed how heads rolled one morning when I was in the UAW education department and saw education director Victor Reuther and his assistant Joe Kowalski draw up a list of staff people scheduled to be purged from that department. By the end of 1947 the Reuther forces were in complete control of communications, finances, and staff resources of the UAW. "There followed a mopping up operation in which the administration brought to bear the full power of the international union—sometimes exceeding its constitutional authority—against hard core opposition locals and their leaders," says Stieber. A member of Packard Local 190 sang the swan song for local union oppositionists in these words:

I come from a local that has always been militant, and when we don't agree with people even in high places we say so. The result has been for the past several years that every time the other officers and myself have run for election in Packard we have not only had to face the ordinary politics of the local union, but, what is inexcusable, we had to face the interference of international representatives. Talk about fighting on two fronts—we have done it for three years and it has not availed. But I think this is basically wrong. When leaders have the power that rests in the hands of the International, the least they can do is to keep their hands off the contests of the little guys who do not threaten them in the local union.

Thanks to such exercise of international power, opposition in locals was stamped out so successfully that by 1951 the delegations of local after local voted 100 percent for the administration's policies.

Could the UAW be More Democratic?

Stieber suggests changes which would make the UAW more democratic: amend convention procedures to give the delegates a voice in the selection of convention committees; ease the requirement for a roll call vote; relax the constitutional requirement that local publications conform to international policies; open the international newspaper to opposition views; accord a more tolerant attitude toward opposition movements at all levels of the international hierarchy; make explicit in the constitution the right to criticize international and local union officers and their policies, the right to form and finance political groups within the union, and the right to communicate for political purposes with local unions and members.

Crackdown

Over a century ago the British reformer Robert Owen believed he could soften the hearts of his fellow capitalists by appealing to them to stop the frightful exploitation of their factory workers and voluntarily raise wages and humanize working conditions. His utopian appeal fell on deaf ears. To expect a labor hierarchy to voluntarily surrender its bureaucratic control is likewise utopian. To believe that an entrenched labor bureaucracy can be persuaded to "accord a more tolerant attitude toward opposition movements" is sheer wishful thinking. For example, such an opposition group in Detroit regularly issues shop papers similar to those put out by the Communist Party in the late 1920s and early 1930s. Titled *Spark*, these rebel papers expose working conditions in auto plants. *Spark* is also published in printed tabloid form. The September 1973 issue reported how UAW officials crushed a wildcat strike at Chrysler in the most intolerant and vindictive manner:

UAW Goons Smash Wildcat

Within one month's time, Chrysler workers shut down three Detroit plants by strong wildcats. The UAW, which supposedly represents these workers, did its best to crush all three strikes.

At Jefferson Assembly Plant, two workers locked themselves in the electrical cage and then turned off the power. They were surrounded and defended by hundreds of their co-workers. Chrysler had made the mistake of leaving the other workers in the plant.

So the plant guards and Detroit cops couldn't get to the two men easily. And the two were in an area with much valuable and essential equipment. As a result, Chrysler was forced to give in to the demands of hundreds of workers, who had already gone through all the union procedures in trying to get rid of a general foreman. The foreman was a racist and abusive to workers in Chrysler's mad drive to speed up production.

The workers won a small victory when the company agreed in writing to fire the foreman and not penalize anyone involved in the shutdown. But even that was too much for the UAW officials. They are feeling too uptight to allow the workers to feel they can influence the work situation. International Vice President Doug Frazer even had to bawl out Chrysler for its handling of the Jefferson situation and said that the company was *wrong in giving in to the workers!*

Ten Day-Wildcat

Shortly afterward, workers at the Chrysler Forge plant wildcatted for ten days because many workers were fired and several injured. The UAW local had only nine grievances on file. And yet, the Forge workers were so fed up that *they were willing to give up hundreds of dollars of pay for the fight*. The union played its usual tricks to get the workers back on the job. The UAW threatened them and made it clear that the International would do everything necessary to break the strike.

At the same time, the International promised to authorize a strike if the workers went back. The Local split 50–50 in voting to continue the shutdown. But the UAW called workers back to work and opened a way through the picket line with International representatives.

Of course, now that workers have gone back, there has been no strike authorized. And the leaders of the walkout are out on the street.

Worst Betrayal

But the worst betrayal by UAW officials came at the Mack Avenue Stamping plant. Chrysler fired five workers for leading a fight to get more fans. Several of the fired workers tried to get support from other workers by calling them to Department 9780, welding. Guards attacked the two. Other workers came to their defense, and a sitdown strike began. Chrysler had learned a lesson at Jefferson and quickly cleared the plant by telling everyone that there was a bomb in the plant. Most people left, without even knowing that hundreds of workers were sitting down in the welding department.

That was how it started. But the real cause was horrible working conditions. Workers at Mack faced constant speed-up, were killed and injured by machinery, and saw stewards fired for trying to defend them. Just like at other plants, conditions became unbearable for human beings to work under. *And the UAW was failing to protect the membership.*

UAW Strike Breakers

So workers held out inside the Mack plant for about 30 hours, until the Detroit cops went in and dragged them out. Then several hundred workers went to the Local 212 hall and voted almost unanimously to throw up picket lines and continue the strike.

The strikers were solid, and both Chrysler and the UAW International understood that the other Mack workers would not cross the lines. Then the UAW International turned to open strikebreaking.

First they used the TV and radio to spread lies about the sit-down strike. They claimed that very few workers were involved, that it was all the work of "outside agitators." They told Chrysler to use whatever means were necessary to break the strike.

But Chrysler was still unwilling to call in the workers it had sent home, because of the hundreds of pickets at the plant gates. So the UAW International rounded up a force of 700 bureaucrats, mostly from Chrysler locals, to act as strikebreakers. This official UAW goon squad was armed with sticks, canes, pipes, and even knives. It broke up the picket lines, threatened and roughed up the pickets and beat up some of them.

And these strikebreakers were paid for their work out of workers' dues! The goons were given lost time money, expenses, and free meals—all paid for by the different locals. The UAW bureaucrats made it absolutely clear which side of the class line they stand on. They are with the bosses 100 percent—and then some.

Len De Caux on Reuther

"Up to 1938, Reuther was a radical united-fronter, in the spirit of the CIO uprising. Then he grasped anti-communism as a grappling hook to climb to power in UAW; he became prime mover for an antileftist purge and split in CIO, and for years one of the country's leading Cold Warriors," writes Len De Caux in his *Labor Radical, a Personal History.*

I hope that a qualified labor scholar will soon produce a definitive study of the impact on the American labor movement made by the Cold War and the anti-communist hysteria during the McCarthy period. Such an objective study should show that the Reuther forces could never have achieved their solid control over the UAW without the handy weapon of Cold War anti-communism. Just as the CIO was able to expel left-wing unions from its fold, so the UAW was able to drive left-wingers (Communist Party-liners and their followers) from key positions in the International and in UAW locals.

I think Len De Caux is quite right in saying that Reuther "mounted the driver's seat of a Cold War steamroller, heading for total control of a once-uncontrolled union." Extreme right-wing groups like the Associated Catholic Trade Unionists were helped by Reuther and his associates—including some in the Socialist Party—to conduct a steady campaign of Red-baiting against union opponents. More than once did I hear Walter Reuther tell an audience that his union defeated Communists and fellow travelers by purely democratic means, by force of superior ideas and constructive programs. But I know how the Reuther people Red-baited their opponents in union local elections; one by one those union members who were tagged "Reds" were defeated when the votes were counted. When I served as education director in Local 212, not only were Communist Party-liners Red-baited, but so were known members of the Socialist Workers Party (Trotskyites) and their supporters when they ran for election.

Labor Radical is heavily weighted with Communist Party-line bias. The good guys are "left-wingers" (radicals) and the bad guys are "right-wingers" (reactionaries). In one place De Caux says Reuther looked to the left "like the smart demogogic opportunist best qualified to lead the workers into accommodation with the American capitalist expansionism."

Nowhere does De Caux explain how the Communist Party did all in its power to lead the workers into accommodation with American capitalism during the period when the Communist Party's Earl Browder hailed communism as "twentieth-century Americanism." In the UAW we used to joke about those incongruous terms: "left wing" and "right wing". During World War II the so-called right-wingers fought bitterly to prevent the Communists and their backers from turning the UAW into a Russian type labor organization—a glorified, compulsory company union. Had the Communists had their way, the big auto companies would have been able to restore incentive pay, increase speedup at will, fire militants who rebelled against surrendering all union gains for the war effort. It was not only Red-baiting that undermined the influence of the Communists in the CIO, especially in the UAW. In the eyes of independent UAW militants, the Communists behaved like fish out of water because of their political turns and twists and sommersaults. And many of those independent militants were repelled by the CP's Machiavellian tactics in interunion struggles. As the leading labor journalist in the CIO from the days of the big sit-down strikes until 1947, when he was fired by Philip Murray during the Red purges, De Caux most certainly must have known how the CP forces resorted to any and all means, however unscrupulous, to achieve their ends.

Labor Radical is the story of the CIO written by a competent labor journalist who has a flair for sharp comment and striking phrase. He has something of the novelist's bent for depicting character, as when he describes men like Lewis, Hillman, Reuther, and other leaders who shaped the CIO. His book views the CIO from the top. Like so many other labor books, De Caux's volume identifies the union movement with the hierarchy. And the outstanding leaders who were high in CIO leadership—Lewis, Hillman, Murray, Reuther, Carey, Curran, Quill, and a host of others—are evaluated in terms of the CP line.

William Serrin on the UAW

The Company and the Union deals, as the title implies, as much with General Motors as with the UAW. I have been told that when the book first appeared it infuriated the UAW hierarchy and those union staff members who took the trouble to read it. And UAW apologists who denounced Serrin for what they said was his "uncritical and irresponsible piece of labor writing" were themselves uncritical and irresponsible in their denunciation; according to them the book is utterly worthless as a study of the relationship between the UAW and the auto corporations.

I think it is a valuable book, not for what it proves or doesn't prove, but because of the questions it raises with respect to its central theme: the relationship between the company and the union is not one of antagonism but a self-serving partnership that is advantageous to both institutions. To amplify this theme, Serrin explores the developments of the 1970 General Motors strike, and by unraveling the intricacies of the bargaining negotiations he comes to the conclusion that nobody lost, both sides won, and General Motors and the UAW have a greater community of interest than of conflict.

I am not qualified to pass judgment on what Serrin tells us about the growth of General Motors and the careers of men who shaped it into the world's largest industrial corporation. Nor do I feel qualified to evaluate his interpretation of what took place at the bargaining sessions, for I was not there. Nor am I able to appraise the author's claim that the 1970 General Motors strike played itself out step by step until it reached a settlement that served none but those who negotiated it. I would not accept his claim as an established fact but as a challenging hypothesis—a hypothesis that needs further careful exploration and testing.

In my opinion the book has some glaring weaknesses. To cite one: several times Serrin correctly observes that the corporation heads are motivated by an all-consuming drive to maximize profits on invested capital; then at the end of the book he advances the unbelievably naive theory that "what is needed are sensitive, humanistic men in positions of power at General Motors . . . for that is the key, sensitivity and humanism." Since when have sensitivity and humanism been compatible with maximizing profits?

But the author is not naive when he throws the spotlight on the UAW's flagrant shortcomings—its failure to attack such problems as war, racism, sex discrimination, highway safety, factory safety, housing, and environmental pollution. "It was the sons of the working men who were being claimed by the war in Vietnam, but the UAW did not attack the war until attacking the war was acceptable. Freeways are axing through the neighborhoods of the working class, not rich or well-to-do, but the UAW has not attacked freeways."

When making these charges against the UAW leadership, Serrin is on safe ground. Consider the union's stand on the Vietnam war. The UAW, like the AFL-CIO, is a prop of the Democratic Party. When President Johnson escalated the war and the American military rained genocidal destruction on men, women, and children in Vietnamese villages, the UAW took no official stand against the war. UAW Secretary-Treasurer Emil Mazey spoke at antiwar rallies and minced no words when condemning United States policy in Indochina. But the politically initiated people in the UAW suspected that Walter Reuther kept a checkrein on Emil's antiwar activities; when Lyndon Johnson flipped the whip, Walter and his executive board advised Emil to "cool it." But when America's corporate and political rulers decided that the country could no longer afford the staggering drain of money and resources plus mounting dissension at home—then the war became increasingly unpopular, even in high places, and the Nixon administration called for "peace with honor." War hawks turned into doves overnight. Even UAW's newly elected President Woodcock jumped on the bandwagon and publicly announced that he had been wrong in supporting the war and Mazey had been right in opposing it.

Racism

Serrin is correct in contending that the UAW does little to attack racism. Many times I have heard former radicals, now on the union payroll, claim that the union's leadership is more progressive than the ranks are on the race question and much more determined to combat discrimination. People who argue this way mistake rhetoric for practice. UAW leaders can make stirring speeches about ending race prejudice, but when confronted with the problem they tread warily, fearing a white backlash. I know committeemen who took a firm stand in favor of allowing blacks the right to be promoted to better jobs in line with seniority. Those committeemen were defeated by their white fellow workers who dubbed them "nigger lovers." While education director of Local 212, I was often told by the local's white politicians: "The first rule for winning an election is never to stick out your neck on the race problem."

Serrin quotes a black auto worker: "We're still on the plantation. That's what the plant is—short for plantation." And another black worker laments: "Nobody does anything for us, not the company, not the union." How many times have I heard that same lament expressed in different words when I worked at Dodge, Ford, and Briggs locals!

Telling It Like It Is

I am always amused when union officials and their supporters accuse rank and file caucus leaders and other critics of the union of being "throwbacks to the radical thirties." When those rebel caucus leaders expose the highhanded actions of the leadership and when they call for more democracy at the local level, they are told: "The turbulent thirties are dead; you can't bring them back again!" Well, it's not a question of bringing back the thirties; it's a question of seeing the relationship between the union and the corporation in realistic terms and telling it the way it is.

During the 1936–37 sit-down strikes the auto barons were determined to smash the fledgling UAW. Today, as Serrin points out, the corporation needs the union as much as the union needs the corporation. During the thirties the UAW was a crusade, run by the men and women who composed it; today it is run from the top down. In the thirties the negotiating committees, along with the international union, played a vital role in negotiations; today the negotiating committee people are sounding boards for the top leadership; "they provide the image to give the negotiations the smell of democracy," says Serrin. In the thirties auto workers struggled to break down the harsh disciplinarian rules arbitrarily imposed by the companies and enforced by hard-boiled supervisors and straw bosses; today, as William Carr, UAW Local 160 president, shrewdly observes: "The union plays quite a role in restraining working people in our society. There is a flow between the corporation and the International to keep the corporation running—the International is a satellite of the corporation. Solidarity for the sake of solidarity does not serve the union at all."

In the thirties, when the steward had power at the shop level, the union was able to improve job conditions and reduce line speeds; today, for all the UAW's liberalism and Woodcock's rhetoric, the assembly lines remain plodding, monotonous, pace-driving treadmills.

In saying all this I am not hankering after the thirties; I am simply stating facts that can be documented.

Bibliography

Blackwood, George. *The United Automobile Workers of America 1935–1951.* Ph.D. dissertation, Detroit: Wayne State University Archives, 1951.

De Caux, Len. *Labor Radical, A Personal History.* Boston: Beacon Press, 1970.

Dunn, Robert W. *Labor and Automobiles.* New York: International Publishers, 1929.

Fine, Sidney. *Origins of the United Automobile Workers.* Ann Arbor: University of Michigan Press, 1958.

———. *Sit-Down—The General Motors Strike of 1936–37.* Ann Arbor: University of Michigan Press, 1969.

———. *The Automobile Under the Blue Eagle.* Ann Arbor: University of Michigan Press, 1963.

Howe, Irving, and Widick, B.J. *The UAW and Walter Reuther.* New York: Random House, 1948.

Levinson, Edward. *Labor on the March.* New York: Harper & Brothers, 1938.

———. *Rise of the Auto Workers.* Detroit: UAW Education Department, n.d.

Lynd, Staughton, and Lynd, Alice. *Rank and File—Personal Histories by Working Class Organizers.* Boston: Beacon Press, 1973.

Michigan History. Volume 52, Number 3, Michigan Department of State, Fall 1973.

Muste, A.J. *Essays of A. J. Muste.* Edited by Nat Hentoff. New York: Simon and Schuster, 1967.

———. *The Automobile Industry and Organized Labor.* Baltimore: Christian Social Justice Fund, n.d.

Serrin, William. *The Company and the Union.* New York: Alfred A. Knopf, 1973.

Stieber, Jack. *Governing the UAW.* New York: John Wiley and Sons, 1962.

Terkel, Studs. *Hard Times.* New York: Random House, 1970.

Widick, B.J. *Detroit—City of Race and Class Violence.* Chicago: Quadrangle Books, 1972.

(243)   X5926

LIPPINCOTT LIBRARY

This material is due on date stamped.
Fines are charged for each late item.

MAY   3 1976

CANCELLED OCT 0 7 1983

MAY 19 1976   LIPPINCOTT
               LIPPINCOTT
June 28   MAY 11 1987
               APR 17 1987
July 9   CANCELLED

F P D   JHW

CANCELLED JUL 2 7 1976

OCT 1 4 1977

CANCELLED 1977

VAN PELT

APR 29 1997

APR 25 1997

M-445